totally luscious CUPCAKES

Inspirational recipes for every occasion and taste

Benjamin Wong

Marshall Cavendish
Cuisine

Copyright © 2023 Marshall Cavendish International (Asia) Private Limited

First published as *Cupcakes with Attitude*, 2012
This new edition, 2023

Published by Marshall Cavendish Cuisine
An imprint of Marshall Cavendish International

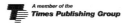

All rights reserved

No part of this publication may be reproduced, stored in a retrieval system or transmitted, in any form or by any means, electronic, mechanical, photocopying, recording or otherwise, without the prior permission of the copyright owner. Requests for permission should be addressed to the Publisher, Marshall Cavendish International (Asia) Private Limited, 1 New Industrial Road, Singapore 536196. Tel: (65) 6213 9300
E-mail: genref@sg.marshallcavendish.com Website: www.marshallcavendish.com

Limits of Liability/Disclaimer of Warranty: The Author and Publisher of this book have used their best efforts in preparing this book. The parties make no representation or warranties with respect to the contents of this book and are not responsible for the outcome of any recipe in this book. While the Publisher has reviewed each recipe carefully, the reader may not always achieve the results desired due to variations in ingredients, cooking temperatures and individual cooking abilities. The Publisher shall in no event be liable for any loss of profit or any other commercial damage, including but not limited to special, incidental, consequential, or other damages.

Other Marshall Cavendish Offices:
Marshall Cavendish Corporation, 800 Westchester Ave, Suite N-641, Rye Brook, NY 10573, USA • Marshall Cavendish International (Thailand) Co Ltd, 253 Asoke, 16th Floor, Sukhumvit 21 Road, Klongtoey Nua, Wattana, Bangkok 10110, Thailand • Marshall Cavendish (Malaysia) Sdn Bhd, Times Subang, Lot 46, Subang Hi-Tech Industrial Park, Batu Tiga, 40000 Shah Alam, Selangor Darul Ehsan, Malaysia

Marshall Cavendish is a trademark of Times Publishing Limited

National Library Board, Singapore Cataloguing-in-Publication Data

Name(s): Wong, Benjamin (Baker).
Title: Totally luscious cupcakes : inspirational recipes for every occasion and taste / Benjamin Wong.
Description: New edition. | Singapore : Marshall Cavendish Cuisine, 2023. | First published as: Cupcakes with attitude, 2012.
Identifier(s): ISBN 978-981-5084-81-8 (paperback)
Subject(s): LCSH: Cupcakes.
Classification: DDC 641.8653--dc23

Printed in Singapore

Photographer: Joshua Tan, Elements By The Box

*This book is dedicated to Dad, Mum and Mark.
Thanks for your love, patience and support,
and for always being there for me.
Thanks for making my life so blessedly wonderful!*

Acknowledgements

This book is made possible by Melvin and Lydia of Marshall Cavendish, so a big THANK YOU is in order!

My editor, the ever reassuring Audrey, was there to make sure I was sane and on time with the deadlines!

A special thanks to the best food photographer in the world—Joshua of Elements By The Box. Well done!

To my family and friends who propelled me to create the many cupcake flavours here, thank you! Your numerous taste-testing and feedback are truly much appreciated. Your discerning taste and dietary requirements are really the inspiration for many recipes here!

Contents

- **07** Introduction
- **09** Before You Start
- **16** Glossary of Ingredients
- **24** The First Move
- **30** Strong and Confident
- **56** Irresistibly Smooth
- **74** Sporty Fit
- **92** Spicy Cool
- **114** Devilishly Debonair
- **144** At the Top
- **168** Weights and Measures

Introduction

For years, I was the occasional baker who was known for baking cakes out of a box, especially on a lazy Sunday afternoon. Yes, I'm talking about those cake mixes in which you just whisk in eggs and butter! The cakes don't taste too bad and the mixes are really easy to use.

In 2008, I took baking classes and was introduced to the joy of baking cupcakes. I experimented with various cupcakes and even developed a few recipes. I held tea parties for friends and offered to bring cupcake desserts to gatherings, soliciting as much feedback as possible.

Before I knew it, I was busy setting up an online bakery! For over two years, I sold cupcakes and fancy cakes to anyone and everyone who enjoyed cupcakes and sweets.

When I tell friends and strangers about my little baking enterprise, they are often amazed that a banker such as myself was able to bake, let alone sell my baked goods! Many say that baking is a science, I beg to differ. Successful baking is a matter of passion, and often, intuition!

Baking is like life. Looking back, I am proud to say that the human spirit is one that is beyond challenge. When we resolve to do anything we choose, there is nothing but achievement and sweet success (pun intended) that awaits!

I am proud to write this book containing recipes that are simple to follow, yet exciting to share and enjoy. These are the cupcakes I would personally bake for the people I love. I have also included alcoholic and unusual flavours not often found elsewhere. The beauty of it all is that you don't need a lot of ingredients and equipment to get started. Many of the things are probably already available in your kitchen!

Above all, this is a book for people who are new to baking and those who are fascinated with cupcakes. I hope this book will give you the confidence to start baking, help you get a sense of what is needed to make great tasting cupcakes and propel you to develop some of your own recipes.

Remember, the secret to great cupcakes are the 3Ps: Practice, Patience and Passion. The only limit is your imagination!

Yours truly,

Benjamin Wong

Before You Start...

know your oven

It is important that you get familiar with your oven and the functions it has to offer. And by this I mean more than reading the instruction manual. You have to experiment with your oven to get the most out of it.

I use a simple conventional oven with heat coming from the upper and lower heating elements.

Depending on your oven, you may need to increase the baking time or adjust the temperature rather than strictly following the instructions given in the recipe.

Some ovens have an automatic fan to circulate the heat evenly. This may speed up or interfere with baking time, as well as how the cupcakes turn out.

Larger ovens allow to you to bake two or three trays of cupcakes at the same time, and this may require you to select the heating elements to be accompanied by the automatic fan. I suggest you follow the instructions given by the oven manufacturer as well as experiment with your oven to ensure you get the best results.

As the cakes near the end of their suggested baking time, look through the glass door of the oven to see if your cakes have risen and are done. Remove the cakes from the oven and test doneness with a toothpick inserted into the centre of the cakes. The toothpick should come out clean. If not, pop the cakes back into the oven to bake further.

where does the baking tray go?

For most conventional ovens, it is best that you position the baking tray at the lowest level or ensure that the cakes are at the centre of the oven.

When baking two or three trays of cupcakes in the oven at the same time, the cupcakes placed on the upper tray tend to bake faster than those on the lower tray as they are closer to the heating element. As such, you may have to swap the trays halfway through the baking time.

I prefer to bake one tray at a time as this allows for evenly baked cakes. Swapping trays in the middle of baking may result in cakes collapsing and not rising properly (this is especially so for big cakes).

to rotate or not to rotate

Depending on the heating element, cupcakes placed at the back of the oven may brown faster than others on the same tray. Some bakers rotate the baking tray halfway through baking; i.e. switching the cupcakes at the front to the back, and vice versa.

I usually rotate the trays when I am baking light-coloured cupcakes to ensure that they are baked evenly and the colour for all the cupcakes is uniform. I rotate the tray about three-quarters into the baking time. For example, if the cupcakes take 25–28 minutes to bake, I rotate the cupcakes after about 20 minutes and leave them inside the oven for the last 5–8 minutes. If the cupcakes are still over-baked or burnt after rotating the baking tray, you may have to lower the oven temperature or shorten the baking time.

If the cupcakes brown evenly in your oven, there is no need to rotate the baking trays.

baking equipment

cake mixer

Many of the recipes in this book require a hand-held cake mixer. Some recipes specifically require a whisk in hand—yes, that's all!

When I was running my online bakery, I survived on a basic cake mixer I bought for about S$50. It was only after nine months that my mum gifted me a heavy-duty stand mixer. So there is really no need to go out and get the most expensive mixer if you are just starting out.

If you have a cake mixer that comes with several attachments, I suggest using the paddle attachment when making cake batters and buttercream, and the whisk attachment for whipping creams and making meringues.

A further note when using a cake mixer: You should always scrape down the sides and bottom of the mixing bowl with a spatula midway through the mixing process to ensure the ingredients are well mixed.

mixing bowls

Even if you already possess a cake mixer that comes with a mixing bowl, it is good to have separate stainless steel mixing bowls. These are really handy around the kitchen, as they will be useful in prep work among other uses. Some bakers prefer mixing bowls made of glass, plastic and other materials; I prefer stainless steel ones as they are durable, hygienic, light and do not break! One big and one small mixing bowl will generally suffice.

whisks

A hand-held whisk can help mix dry ingredients (i.e. flour, baking soda, cocoa powder, etc.) efficiently. In addition, if you are starting out and do not want to splurge on a cake mixer, a hand-held whisk and mixing bowls will be more than sufficient to start your expedition on baking. Needless to say, you will be working those arms!

baking (muffin) trays

These are readily available from supermarkets and speciality stores. Buy the right-sized ones for your oven, but importantly, buy good ones—and when you care for them properly, they can last you for a long time. My trays were handed down from my mum, and I have been using them since!

cupcake liners

The choices are plenty here. You can take your pick, but they must fit the trays you have. I suggest that you purchase both paper liners as well as the foil-laminated ones. Do note that not all cupcake liners are of the same size; so if you prefer to use a certain cupcake liner, you may need to prepare more or less batter and adjust the recipe accordingly.

Waxed muffin liners or cups are also really handy as you don't need a baking tray! Just place the batter-filled waxed liners on a baking sheet or pan and pop them into the oven directly.

ice cream scoops

I use these to divide the cake batter among cupcake liners to ensure the cupcakes are of even sizes.

pouring cups

If the cake batter is very watery (there are a few recipes here with such cake batter), then a pouring cup will be more convenient when dividing cake batter among the cupcake tins or liners. It is efficient and you save on the cleaning and avoid dripping batter everywhere!

measuring equipment

For any aspiring baker, these are important and they help you apportion the needed ingredients:

- Weighing machine—ensure it is on a flat and levelled surface.
- Measuring cups—when measuring out flour and sugar, do not pack down, and use a knife to level the ingredients.
- Measuring spoons—do not pack down the ingredients, and use a knife to level the ingredients you are measuring out.

wire rack

Use these racks for cooling your cupcakes and other baked goods.

spatula

A right-sized spatula is useful for folding whipped cream or flour into cake batter, or scraping down the sides and bottoms of your mixing bowls to ensure that all the cake batter or frosting is used. Get good quality ones that can also be used for melting chocolate or light cooking.

A small (and offset) stainless steel spatula is helpful for spreading frosting over cupcakes. You can use a butter knife or the back of a spoon to do this too.

piping bags and tips

If you wish to get fancy with your frostings, you will need piping bags and tips. (Optional: Use a coupler to secure the piping bag and tip together.)

I prefer disposable piping bags as there is no need to clean up after use. As for piping tips, a simple round or medium-size star tip will suffice. Of course, you may wish to invest in a few more tips to create different elaborate designs on your frostings.

In addition, piping bags can be used for piping batter into muffin trays, especially for batters that are messy and hard to handle.

decorating cupcakes

I have intentionally kept decorating cupcakes simple here. A spoon or small spatula is all that is needed to decorate the cupcakes with the frosting of choice. Practice makes perfect, as they say, and swirling and twirling out impressive frostings is of no exception.

For the adventurous, get ready piping bags and piping tips. Decorating cupcakes can be a fun experience and the kids will definitely enjoy doing this—it is a great exercise to developva sense of achievement in the little ones! Dressing up cakes together with loved ones can be very rewarding too.

storing cupcakes and frostings

cupcakes

Cupcakes can be kept at room temperature or in a cool room. These should stay fresh for 3 days.

Chilling cupcakes in the refrigerator will prolong their shelf life up to a week, but the cakes tend to harden and this is especially so for chocolate cakes. Remove cupcakes from the refrigerator and leave them to reach room temperature before serving.

Cupcakes can also be frozen. Frozen cupcakes can be kept for about 2 weeks.

frostings

If not eaten within the day, frostings made with cream, cream cheese, mascarpone cheese or butter should be kept in the refrigerator to ensure freshness. These can keep up to 1 week.

Frostings made with vegetable shortening can be kept in a bowl, covered with cling wrap, in a cool place for up to 1 week.

If using frostings that have been kept aside or refrigerated, whisk with a fork before use. The fluffing will make the frosting easier to work with.

one final note...

Before you start baking, read through the recipes such that you understand what is needed. Have all the ingredients ready and prepare all the necessary equipment. This way, you don't spend extra time looking for ingredients and equipment—and you avoid prolonging mixing times, which can affect the outcome of the cakes.

Glossary of Ingredients

butter

Butter is made of cream or butterfat and water. The best butter for baking should have at least 80% cream—the higher the fat content, the more moist (and tastier) the cakes will be. Use unsalted butter as it will be fresher than salted ones and thus will not alter the taste of the cakes.

As a healthier alternative, butter may be substituted with ingredients like margarine or non-dairy fat, but these may not give you the resultant taste that you want.

When incorporating into cake batter, butter should be at room temperature so it has a soft consistency which can be easily blended.

However, cold butter is best for making buttercreams and frostings. Take it out of the refrigerator 10–15 minutes before using.

caster sugar

Not all sugars are equal. I prefer caster sugar as it blends or dissolves faster into the butter than fine sugar. If you only have fine or granulated sugar at home, that will be fine as well.

For the health conscious, agave nectar or syrup can be used in place of sugar. However, the resultant texture and volume of the cakes will be different. Agave is believed to have a lower glycemic index than sugar, and thus deemed a healthier option. Do note that agave is sweeter than sugar; the ratio of agave to sugar is NOT 1:1; usually, every 100 g (3$^1/_2$ oz) sugar may be substituted with 60 g (2 oz) or less of agave nectar or syrup. Read the labels of the agave you are using to ascertain the correct substitute ratio.

brown sugar

Brown sugar is a combination of sugar and molasses. The darker the sugar, the higher the molasses content. What I like about using brown sugar is that it lends a treacle-like flavour to cupcakes. If you prefer, you can substitute brown sugar with white or caster sugar and vice versa.

icing (confectioner's) sugar

This is granulated sugar ground to a very fine powder with cornflour (cornstarch) added. It is used in frostings and buttercreams to give them shape and volume. The cornflour in the sugar maintains the shape of the frostings and buttercreams. Icing sugar tends to clump, so always sift it before using to ensure easier blending with butter, cream or vegetable shortening.

vegetable shortening

Vegetable shortening can be used for baking, and some recipes call for this rather than butter. It is great for making buttercreams and frostings, and it can withstand warm and humid weather better than butter. Vegetable shortening is white, and the resultant frostings are open for colouring and flavouring. What's great about this ingredients is that it has little or no trans-fat, and does not need to be kept in the refrigerator.

eggs

Eggs are very crucial to baking. Egg whites have a leavening effect—when beaten at high speed it tends to foam and rise to form soft peaks, which is folded into the batter to give cakes a light and fluffy texture. Egg yolks contain fat and lend a smooth, rich texture to cakes.

For a baker, the bigger the eggs the better! Eggs should be at room temperature before use. Using cold eggs in batter can cause shrinkage and affect the cake and its taste.

For health reasons, pregnant women, young children and those who are medically challenged should avoid recipes that use uncooked eggs.

plain (all-purpose) flour

Plain flour is easily available, and produces very decent cakes. If you prefer a finer texture, try using cake flour instead; it has less protein content than most other flours, and can produce cakes of different textures.

Sifting flours before using will also give your cakes a lighter and fluffier texture. You can also experiment with using a combination of plain flour and cake flour in a recipe.

self-raising flour

Many of the recipes here use self-raising flour. It is convenient and takes the guess work out of deciding how much baking powder or baking soda to use.

baking powder

Owing to the chemical content, baking powder aerates cakes (through the addition of carbon dioxide) when it comes into contact with wet ingredients. It also helps cakes to rise when exposed to heat. Baking powder is usually used in recipes where little or no acidic ingredients are added.

Baking powder must be fresh. If not, it does not have any effect on cakes. To test for effectiveness, add $1/4$ tsp baking powder to 125 ml (4 fl oz / $1/2$ cup) hot water. Bubbles should form in the water instantly.

baking soda (bicarbonate of soda)

Baking soda aerates cakes and helps them rise. It is often used in recipes where there are acidic ingredients such as buttermilk, fruit juice and sour cream.

You should bake the cake batter soon after the baking soda is added to wet ingredients as the batter will start to rise. Baking powder and baking soda are NOT interchangeable.

Like baking powder, baking soda should be fresh. To test for effectiveness, add $1/4$ tsp baking powder to 125 ml (4 fl oz / $1/2$ cup) hot water (with $1/4$ tsp white vinegar added). Bubbles should form in the water instantly.

sea salt and table salt

Salt often enhances the taste of cakes and frostings. In terms of taste, there is little or no difference between sea salt and table salt. Sea salt, being coarser, may be lighter than table salt for any given amount. If you choose to substitute one for the other in a recipe, use slightly more sea salt than table salt.

cocoa powder

Cocoa powder is made by removing three-quarters of cocoa butter content. The remaining cocoa solids are then finely ground to make cocoa powder. Cocoa powder gives cakes an intense and deep flavour as compared to using solid chocolate alone. I recommend sifting cocoa powder before use as it tends to clump.

All recipes here use unsweetened cocoa powder.

baking chocolate

Chocolate comes in bars, blocks or drops. I prefer using drops which does not require chopping and is easier to melt.

Always use the best chocolate you can afford. Good quality baking chocolate or couverture has higher cocoa butter content (preferably over 30%), which makes melting easier. It also imparts a creamy flavour to cakes and frostings.

Generally, there are three types of chocolate: Milk, semi-sweet and bitter. The difference lies in the percentage of cocoa solids, milk content and sugar. For convenient and easy reference, I have broadly classified the three types of chocolate as:

- Milk chocolate—cocoa solids less than 50%
- Semi-sweet chocolate—cocoa solids between 50% and 70%
- Bitter-sweet chocolate—cocoa solids more than 70%

From my experience, semi-sweet chocolate has wide gastronomical appeal. Anything below 50% tastes of milk chocolate. Anything with cocoa solids of 70% and above might be bitter, given the lesser sugar content, and could be an acquired taste.

Melting chocolate should be done via a double boiler or bain-marie. Melt chocolate couverture in a metal bowl placed over a pot of boiling water, and stir with a wooden spoon. Never melt chocolate placed over direct heat as it burns easily.

When a recipe calls for chocolate couverture, it should not be substituted with chocolate chips. Chocolate chips contain less cocoa butter and are designed to retain their shape while baking, and hence will not melt properly, thus affecting the texture of the cakes and frostings.

white chocolate couverture

White chocolate is essentially milk, sugar and cocoa butter. Cocoa solids are not added at all. Good quality white chocolate couverture should contain at least 20% cocoa butter. Like milk, semi-sweet and dark chocolate couverture, melting white chocolate should be done via a double boiler or bain-marie.

milk

Use full cream milk at all times when baking the cupcakes featured in this book. The fat content will ensure that the cakes will taste their best. If substituting full cream milk with low fat or soy versions, be prepared for a taste compromise.

buttermilk

This can be made at home—there is no need to go out and buy it. Combine 250 ml (8 fl oz / 1 cup) milk and 1 Tbsp white vinegar and stir well. Let it sit for about 5 minutes before use.

heavy cream

Given its fat content of over 36%, it lends a creamy and moist texture to cakes. It can be labelled as whipping cream or double cream, and can contain up to or more than 40% butter fat.

It has a heavier texture than topping cream (non-diary whipping cream—see next). To whip, pour desired amount of heavy cream into a chilled metal bowl and whisk at high speed. Do not overbeat, lest the cream becomes grainy.

Optional: Add 1 Tbsp icing (confectioner's) sugar for every 250 g (9 oz) heavy cream. Icing sugar helps to stabilise the cream. The higher the fat content, the easier to whip the cream up to form. Once cream has fluffed up and is ready for use, flavour as desired.

For consistency throughout the book, I shall refer to this as heavy cream or whipped heavy cream.

topping cream (non-dairy whipping cream)

This is light in texture and easy to whip up to a nice generous volume, and produces really white and glossy frostings. Topping cream is essentially made up of hydrogenated vegetable oils, fructose and skimmed milk powder. Note that this usually contains casein, a milk derivative. The cream, while sweetened already, does need to be flavoured accordingly.

This is suitable for making frostings after brisk whisking in a chilled bowl. Take this out of the refrigerator only when you are ready to use it; the cream should be as cold as possible.

Whip the cream until soft peaks form, and it should appear glossy and moist, which makes it easy to use. If you whip the cream for a longer time, stiff peaks will form and this is ideal for making mousse.

For consistency throughout the book, I shall refer to this as topping cream.

sour cream

This is essentially cream fermented with lactic acid. Sour cream is mildly sour and adds good taste to sweet cakes. The fat content (of about 20% butterfat) in the sour cream gives cakes a smooth texture.

Yoghurt may be used in place of sour cream. However, yoghurt has a higher water content and less fat, which could result in a different taste. The texture could also be compromised.

extracts, essences and flavourings

I like to use organic vanilla extract rather than its essence. If using essence, use slightly less than extract. If too much extract or essence is used, the cakes and frostings may turn out slightly bitter. For those who like using fresh vanilla pods, the scrapped seeds from one vanilla pod should be equivalent to 1 tsp vanilla extract.

Use edible citrus oils (organic, if possible) such as orange and lemon, instead of bottled essences. They give cakes a more intense taste. Add freshly squeezed juices (and their pulp, if any) into cakes and frostings to impart a more authentic flavour.

essential oils

Bottled flavourings are convenient but I prefer to use naturally harvested and therapeutic-grade essential oils. Essential oils of peppermint, lemon, lemongrass, orange and rose (just to name a few) can be used in your cupcakes and frostings (even in your cooking). They are really convenient when you want to add intense taste and flavours, and a few drops go a long way!

Just note that NOT all essential oils are created equal, and many are only suitable for diffusion and not edible. Some manufacturers include additives and fillers which may make them unsuitable for ingestion. I use Young Living essential oils, and the essential oils featured in the recipes here are all safe for consumption.

As a general rule, approximately 3–5 drops of Young Living essential oil can replace 1 tsp bottled flavouring; i.e. 3 drops of peppermint essential oil can replace 1 tsp peppermint flavouring. This also applies to ground spices such as cinnamon, clove and nutmeg, which can be replaced by their respective essential oils. Add a few more drops if you like a stronger taste.

alcohol and spirits

Using alcohol and spirits in cakes can be exciting but tricky. As the heat in the oven tends to evaporate the alcohol in the batter, the residual taste of the alcohol can be insignificant after baking.

In general, dark-coloured alcohol has a slightly higher chance of surviving the baking process compared to lighter-coloured alcohol. Nonetheless, subjecting alcohol and spirits to the baking process is not ideal.

My preference is to (i) drizzle the baked cakes with your chosen alcohol, (ii) soak fruits with alcohol and use the fruits in your cakes, and/or (iii) use alcohol in your frostings, which are not subjected to heat during the preparation process.

If drizzling alcohol over the cakes, use a toothpick to pierce several deep holes into the cakes while they are still warm. Using a spoon, drizzle the required amount of alcohol over the warm cakes. Let cakes cool thoroughly before frosting. If the cake is denser (such as the Tiramsu Cupcakes), consider using a syringe to inject the alcohol into the cakes, as a mere drizzle may not allow the alcohol to penetrate the cake completely.

To enhance the effects of drizzling alcohol over cakes, consider using a syrup. To make a syrup, heat an equal amount of water and caster or brown sugar, and let it simmer a bit to ensure the sugars are completely melted; the syrup should be of pouring consistency. Remove from heat and allow to cool for a bit before adding your choice of alcohol. While this ensures better retention of alcohol taste, the resultant cakes will be sweeter. You have the choice of reducing the sugar content in the cake batter.

Soaking fresh and preserved fruits in alcohol (preferably overnight) is another option. Fold the alcohol-soaked fruits into your cake batter. The darker your fruits are (such as raisins, prunes, etc.), the better they can retain the alcohols and their flavours in the baking process.

The easiest way is to use alcohol and spirits in frostings, as no heat is involved in the preparation process. Instead of using water to thin buttercreams and frostings during the mixing process, use your chosen alcohol.

The First Move

*the foundation to baking
great tasting cupcakes*

plain cupcakes 26
chocolate cupcakes 28

Plain Cupcakes makes 12 cupcakes

Unsalted butter 125 g (4½ oz)

Caster sugar 125 g (4½ oz)

Eggs 2, lightly beaten

Vanilla extract (optional) 1 tsp

Salt (optional) a pinch

Self-raising flour 125 g (4½ oz), sifted

Full cream milk (optional) 2 Tbsp

1. Preheat oven to 180°C (350°F). Line muffin tray with cupcake liners.
2. Cream butter in an electric mixer for a few minutes. Gradually add sugar and continue to beat until well combined.
3. Add eggs and beat until mixture is well blended, light and fluffy.
4. Add vanilla extract and salt if using and mix well.
5. Add flour and continue to beat until well mixed. Stop immediately once all the flour has been mixed well into the batter.
6. Add milk if using and mix well.
7. Spoon batter into cupcake liners until three-quarters full. Bake for 20–25 minutes.
8. When cupcakes are done, remove from the oven and leave cupcakes in muffin tray for 5 minutes.
9. Remove cupcakes from tray and place on a wire rack to cool completely before frosting.

These plain cupcakes form the base of many recipes here. You can use this recipe as a starting point should you choose to experiment with different or unusual flavours.

Chocolate Cupcakes makes 12 cupcakes

Self-raising flour 125 g (4½ oz)

Cocoa powder 2 Tbsp

Unsalted butter 125 g (4½ oz)

Caster sugar 125 g (4½ oz)

Eggs 2, lightly beaten

Vanilla extract 1 tsp

Full cream milk (optional) 2 Tbsp

1. Preheat oven to 180°C (350°F). Line muffin tray with cupcake liners.
2. Sift flour and cocoa powder together twice. Set aside.
3. Cream butter in an electric mixer for a few minutes. Gradually add sugar and continue to beat until well combined.
4. Add eggs and beat until mixture is well blended, light and fluffy.
5. Add vanilla extract and mix well.
6. Add flour mixture prepared in step 2 and continue to beat until well mixed. Stop immediately once all the flour has been mixed well into the batter.
7. Add milk if using and mix well.
8. Spoon batter into cupcake liners until three-quarters full. Bake for 20–25 minutes.
9. When cupcakes are done, remove from the oven and let cupcakes sit in the muffin tray for 5 minutes.
10. Remove cupcakes from tray and place on a wire rack to cool completely before frosting.

Note

- For a more chocolaty taste, add up to 3 Tbsp cocoa powder to the batter.
- Sifting flour and cocoa powder will render a lighter cupcake.
- Always sift cocoa powder before use.
- In place of cocoa powder, you can fold 50 g (1⅔ oz) melted chocolate of your choice into the batter. Mix well before spooning the batter into the cupcake liners.

No fuss chocolaty goodness! You can frost these little cakes with any topping that takes your fancy.

strongly flavoured cupcakes made with chocolate, cheese and other robust ingredients

stone works cupcakes	32
chocolate addiction	34
choco-mint cupcakes	36
chocolate banana cupcakes	38
honey rosemary cupcakes	40
coffee walnut cupcakes	42
MJ cupcakes	44
tiramisu cupcakes	47
tiramisu cake pops	48
Coca-Cola cupcakes	51
ham and cheese cupcakes	52
chocolate chip cake pops	54

Stone Works Cupcakes *makes 12 cupcakes*

Unsalted butter 125 g (4½ oz)

Caster sugar 125 g (4½ oz)

Eggs 2, lightly beaten

Vanilla extract 1 tsp

Full cream milk 2 Tbsp

Self-raising flour 125 g (4½ oz)

Cocoa powder 1½ Tbsp, sifted

TOPPING

Chocolate buttercream (page 156) *or* **dark chocolate ganache** (page 146) *or* **icing (confectioner's) sugar**

1. Preheat oven to 180°C (350°F). Line muffin tray with cupcake liners.
2. Cream butter in an electric mixer for a few minutes. Gradually add sugar and continue to beat until well combined.
3. Add eggs and beat until mixture is well blended, light and fluffy.
4. Add vanilla extract and milk. Mix well.
5. Add flour and continue to beat until well mixed. Stop immediately once all the flour has been mixed well into the batter.
6. Measure out one-third of the batter and place in a separate bowl. Add cocoa powder and mix well using a spatula. (Optional: Add 1–2 Tbsp milk into batter such that it is of spreadable consistency.)
7. Spoon alternating layers of vanilla and chocolate batter into cupcake liners until three-quarters full. Using a toothpick or tip of a paring knife, draw swirls in the batter. Bake for 20–25 minutes. Remove from oven and let cupcakes sit in the muffin tray for 5 minutes.
8. Remove cupcakes from tray and place on a wire rack to cool completely before frosting.
9. Spread a thick layer of chocolate buttercream over the cupcakes before serving. Alternatively, top with dark chocolate ganache or simply dust icing sugar over the cupcakes.

A marble chocolate cupcake that will impress any day!

Chocolate Addiction makes 15 cupcakes

Sugar 225 g (8 oz)

Plain (all-purpose) flour 130 g (4$^{2}/_{3}$ oz)

Cocoa powder 60 g (2 oz), sifted

Baking powder $^{3}/_{4}$ tsp

Baking soda $^{3}/_{4}$ tsp

Salt $^{1}/_{2}$ tsp

Egg 1

Full cream milk 125 ml (4 fl oz / $^{1}/_{2}$ cup)

Vegetable oil 4 Tbsp

Vanilla extract 1 tsp

Boiling water 125 ml (4 fl oz / $^{1}/_{2}$ cup)

TOPPING

Dark chocolate ganache (page 146)

Maraschino cherries (optional)

or

Bailey's Irish buttercream (page 154)

Chocolate shavings

1. Preheat oven to 180°C (350°F). Line muffin tray with cupcake liners.
2. Combine sugar, flour, cocoa powder, baking powder, baking soda and salt in a bowl. Mix ingredients well with a whisk.
3. Add egg, milk, oil and vanilla extract and beat using an electric mixer for 2 minutes. Gently stir in boiling water and continue to beat for another 2 minutes. The batter will be watery.
4. Pour batter into cupcake liners until two-thirds full. Bake for 25 minutes or until a toothpick inserted into the centre of the cake comes out clean. Remove from oven and and let cupcakes sit in tray for 5 minutes.
5. Remove cupcakes from tray and place on a wire rack to cool completely before frosting.
6. Pipe dark chocolate ganache on top of cupcakes. Garnish with maraschino cherries if desired. Alternatively, top with Bailey's Irish buttercream and garnish with chocolate shavings.

Note

- As the batter is watery, transfer it to a pouring cup so that it is easier to fill up the cupcake liners.

These simple-to-make chocolate cupcakes are my bestsellers! When paired with dark chocolate ganache, the cupcakes are always a hit with chocolate lovers. Even those who don't like chocolate (for whatever reasons), will be converted to addicts! The cupcakes are especially moist and soft, thanks to the vegetable oil and water used.

Choco-Mint Cupcakes makes 12 cupcakes

Self-raising flour 125 g (4½ oz)

Cocoa powder 2 Tbsp

Unsalted butter 125 g (4½ oz)

Caster sugar 125 g (4½ oz)

Eggs 2, lightly beaten

Vanilla extract 1 tsp

Peppermint essential oil (optional) a few drops

Dark chocolate chips 100 g (3½ oz)

TOPPING

Peppermint buttercream (page 154)

Mini chocolate pearls *or* **chocolate chips**

1. Preheat oven to 180°C (350°F). Line muffin tray with cupcake liners.
2. Sift flour and cocoa powder together and set aside.
3. Cream butter in an electric mixer for a few minutes. Gradually add sugar and continue to beat until well combined.
4. Add eggs and beat until mixture is well blended, light and fluffy.
5. Add vanilla extract and peppermint essential oil if using. Mix well.
6. Add flour mixture prepared in step 2 and continue to beat until well mixed. Stop immediately once all the flour has mixed well into the batter.
7. Fold in chocolate chips using a spatula.
8. Spoon batter into cupcake liners until three-quarters full. Bake for 20–25 minutes. Remove from oven and let cupcakes sit in muffin tray for 5 minutes.
9. Remove cupcakes from tray and place on a wire rack to cool completely before frosting.
10. Pipe ribbons of peppermint buttercream on top of cupcakes. Sprinkle mini chocolate pearls or chocolate chips over topping.

Note

- For more chocolaty cupcakes, add up to 3 Tbsp cocoa powder to the batter.
- You can use ½ tsp peppermint essence in place of peppermint essential oil.

Peppermint essential oil adds an aromatically uplifting dimension to these delectable chocolate chip cupcakes. Friends say these cupcakes are delicious without being heavy. It's like having your cake without feeling guilty!

Chocolate Banana Cupcakes makes 12 cupcakes

Self-raising flour 125 g (4½ oz)

Cocoa powder 2 Tbsp, sifted

Unsalted butter 125 g (4½ oz)

Brown sugar 125 g (4½ oz)

Eggs 2, lightly beaten

Ground cinnamon (optional) 1 tsp

Vanilla essence 1 tsp

Bananas 2, 100–150 g (3½–5⅓ oz), roughly mashed

TOPPING

Sea salt caramel frosting (page 166) *or* **chocolate buttercream** (page 156) *or* **dark chocolate ganache** (page 146)

Banana slices

1. Preheat oven to 180°C (350°F). Line muffin tray with cupcake liners.
2. Sift flour and cocoa powder together in a bowl. Set aside.
3. Beat butter and sugar in an electric mixer at low speed until well blended. Mixture should be light brown and fluffy. Gradually add eggs and mix well.
4. Add flour mixture prepared in step 2, followed by cinnamon if using. Continue to beat until well incorporated.
5. Stir in vanilla essence and gently fold in bananas using a spatula.
6. Spoon batter into cupcake liners until three-quarters full. Bake for 25 minutes. Remove from oven and let cupcakes sit in muffin tray for 5 minutes.
7. Remove cupcakes from tray and place on a wire rack to cool completely before frosting.
8. Spread a thick layer of sea salt caramel frosting on top and garnish with banana slices. Alternatively, chocolate buttercream or dark chocolate ganache will pair nicely with these cupcakes.

Note

- For more chocolaty cupcakes, add up to 3 Tbsp cocoa powder to the batter.
- This recipe can also be used to bake a cake. Just use a 20-cm (8-in) round cake tin lined with parchment paper. Bake for 40 minutes and beyond. It's okay to slightly over-bake the cake, as it is hard to burn. Just remember to take it out of the oven! Test doneness with a toothpick inserted into the centre of the cake—it should come out clean.

Banana lends a moist and yummy texture to these cupcakes, and the addition of cinnamon adds a mouth-watering fragrance.

Honey Rosemary Cupcakes makes 12 cupcakes

Unsalted butter 150 g (5$^1/_3$ oz)
Brown sugar 100 g (3$^1/_2$ oz)
Honey 4 Tbsp
Eggs 3, lightly beaten
Rosemary essential oil (optional) a few drops
Cake flour 150 g (5$^1/_3$ oz)
Chopped fresh rosemary 1 Tbsp

TOPPING
Fresh rosemary sprigs
Royal icing (optional) (page 158)
Orange food colouring (optional)

1. Preheat oven to 180°C (350°F). Line muffin tray with cupcake liners.
2. Cream butter in an electric mixer for a few minutes. Gradually add sugar and honey. Continue to beat until well combined.
3. Add eggs and beat until mixture is well blended, light and fluffy.
4. Add rosemary essential oil if using. Mix well.
5. Add flour and continue to beat until well mixed. Stop immediately once all the flour has been mixed well into the batter.
6. Stir in chopped rosemary using a spatula.
7. Spoon batter into cupcake liners until three-quarters full. Bake for 25 minutes or until cupcakes are golden brown and a toothpick inserted into the centre of the cake comes out clean.
8. Remove from oven and let cupcakes sit in muffin tray for 10 minutes.
9. Remove cupcakes from tray and place on a wire rack to cool completely before frosting.
10. To finish, top with some fresh rosemary sprigs. If you prefer something sweeter, combine royal icing with a few drops of orange food colouring and drizzle over cupcakes before garnishing with rosemary.

Have this for breakfast or a pre-dinner snack!

Coffee Walnut Cupcakes makes 12 cupcakes

Unsalted butter 125 g (4½ oz), softened

Light brown sugar 125 g (4½ oz)

Eggs 2

Vanilla extract 1 tsp

Self-raising flour 125 g (4½ oz), sifted

Coffee granules 1 Tbsp, dissolved in 2 Tbsp hot water

Chopped walnuts 110 g (4 oz)

FOR MOCHA CUPCAKES
Semi-sweet chocolate couverture drops 3 Tbsp

TOPPING
Bailey's Irish buttercream (page 154) *or* **dark chocolate ganache** (page 146)

Walnuts

1. Preheat oven to 180°C (350°F). Line muffin tray with cupcake liners.
2. Cream butter in an electric mixer for a few minutes. Gradually add sugar and continue to beat until well combined.
3. Add eggs and beat until mixture is well blended, light and fluffy.
4. Add vanilla extract and mix well.
5. Add half the flour and beat on low speed. Add coffee and the remaining flour and beat until combined. Do not over beat—stop immediately once the flour and coffee are well mixed into the batter.
6. Fold in walnuts using a spatula. If making mocha cupcakes, fold in chocolate couverture at this point.
7. Spoon batter into cupcake liners until three-quarters full. Bake for 25 minutes or until a toothpick inserted into the centre of cakes comes out clean.
8. Remove from oven and transfer cupcakes to a wire rack to cool completely before frosting.
9. Pipe small dollops of Bailey's Irish buttercream or dark chocolate ganache on top of cupcakes. Garnish with walnuts.

Note

- When making mocha cupcakes, cocoa powder can also be used in place of chocolate couverture. If using, sift 2 Tbsp cocoa powder together with flour before preparing batter, and use a whisk to mix well.
- For convenience, the chocolate couverture should preferably be in drops. If couverture drops are unavailable, melt 50 g (1⅔ oz) chocolate couverture and fold into batter.

These cupcakes add special meaning to the term "coffee break", and are perfect for caffeine junkies who need to stay awake!

MJ Cupcakes makes 12 cupcakes

WITH MELTED CHOCOLATE

Plain (all-purpose) flour 60 g (2 oz)

Cocoa powder 3 Tbsp

Semi-sweet chocolate couverture 225 g (8 oz)

Unsalted butter 125 g (4$\frac{1}{2}$ oz)

Caster sugar 225 g (8 oz)

Salt $\frac{1}{2}$ tsp

Vanilla extract 1 tsp

Eggs 3

Chocolate covered peppermint candy 12 pieces

WITH COCOA POWDER

Plain (all-purpose) flour 160 g (5$\frac{2}{3}$ oz)

Cocoa powder 85 g (3 oz)

Baking powder $\frac{1}{2}$ tsp

Salt $\frac{1}{2}$ tsp

Caster sugar 330 g (11$\frac{3}{4}$ oz)

Butter 185 g (6$\frac{2}{3}$ oz)

Water 2 Tbsp

Eggs 2

Vanilla extract 1 tsp

Chocolate covered peppermint candy 12 pieces

TOPPING

Icing (confectioner's) sugar *or* **vanilla buttercream** (page 154) *or* **white chocolate ganache** (page 148)

WITH MELTED CHOCOLATE

1. Preheat oven to 180°C (350°F). Line muffin tray with cupcake liners.
2. Sift flour and cocoa powder together into a bowl. Set aside.
3. Place chocolate couverture and butter in a metal bowl set over a pan of boiling water. Stir occasionally with a wooden spoon. Once completely melted, remove from heat and set aside to cool.
4. Once cooled, mix in sugar, salt and vanilla extract with a hand-held whisk until well combined.
5. Add eggs one at a time and continue whisking.
6. Using a spatula, fold in flour mixture prepared in step 2 until well combined.
7. Spoon batter into cupcake liners until one-third full. Place 1 candy in the centre of each cupcake. Spoon batter into cupcake liners until two-thirds full.
8. Bake for 30–35 minutes or until a toothpick inserted into the centre of cakes comes out clean. Remove from oven and let cupcakes sit in the muffin tray for 5 minutes. (Cupcakes will be cracked on the top.)
9. Remove cupcakes from tray and place on a wire rack to cool completely before frosting.
10. Dust icing sugar over before serving. Alternatively, top with vanilla buttercream or white chocolate ganache.

WITH COCOA POWDER

1. Preheat oven to 180°C (350°F). Line muffin tray with cupcake liners.
2. Sift flour, cocoa powder, baking powder and salt together. Set aside.
3. Using an electric mixer, whisk sugar, butter and water together on medium speed until well combined.
4. Add eggs and vanilla extract, and continue beating until well combined.
5. Follow steps 6–10 above.

Note

- I have provided two recipes here; one that uses melted chocolate, the other, cocoa powder. While melted chocolate gives a softer and more chocolaty texture, the second recipe is more convenient and produces equally good cupcakes.

MJ stands for Michael Jackson, the iconic superstar who wrote the song Black or White. These cupcakes symbolise the merger of both colours black and white—brownie cupcakes with a mint-white centre. The mint sweet is often a surprise when people bite into the cupcakes; just like the late superstar who never failed to surprise us with his music and performances.

An adaption of the famous Italian dessert—my secret is using good quality rum. Consider using a plastic syringe to inject the alcoholic coffee into the dense cakes. This technique was imparted to me by my cocktail enthusiast of a friend, Kelvin. There is also rum in the frosting!

Tiramisu Cupcakes *makes 18 cupcakes*

Unsalted butter 65 g (2 1/3 oz)

Sugar 225 g (8 oz)

Eggs 3, lightly beaten

Egg yolks from 3 eggs

Vanilla extract 1 tsp

Salt 1/2 tsp

Full cream milk 4 Tbsp

Self-raising flour 185 g (6 2/3 oz), sifted

Hot espresso or any strong coffee 250 ml (8 fl oz / 1 cup)

Rum 3 Tbsp

RUM-SPIKED FROSTING

Heavy cream 500 g (1 lb 1 1/2 oz)

Mascarpone cheese 500 g (1 lb 1 1/2 oz)

Icing (confectioner's) sugar 50 g (1 2/3 oz)

Rum 3 Tbsp

Cocoa powder

1. Preheat oven to 180°C (350°F). Line muffin tray with cupcake liners.
2. Cream butter in an electric mixer for a few minutes. Gradually add sugar and continue to beat until well combined.
3. Add eggs and egg yolks. Beat until mixture is well blended, light and fluffy.
4. Add vanilla extract, salt and milk. Mix well.
5. Add flour and continue to beat until well mixed. Stop immediately once all the flour has been mixed well into the batter.
6. Spoon batter into cupcake liners until three-quarters full. Bake for 20–25 minutes. Remove from oven and let cupcakes sit in muffin tray for 5 minutes.
7. Meanwhile, combine espresso with rum.
8. Pierce several holes in the cupcakes with a toothpick. Using a syringe, inject generous amounts of coffee rum mixture into the cupcakes. Alternatively, you can drizzle the mixture over the cupcakes. Allow to cool completely for at least 30 minutes before frosting.
9. Spoon a generous serving of rum-spiked frosting over the cupcakes. If desired, chill frosted cupcakes in the refrigerator for at least 30 minutes. Dust cocoa powder over frosting just before serving.

RUM-SPIKED FROSTING
1. Prepare whipped cream. In a cake mixer with a whisk attachment, beat heavy cream on high until soft peaks form.
2. In a separate chilled metal bowl, whisk mascarpone cheese with icing sugar using a hand-held electric mixer until sugar has dissolved. Stir in rum.
3. Fold in whipped cream.

Note

- You can use as much as rum as you like in the frosting, but I suggest adding a bit at a time, tasting as you go along. Be careful not to add too much rum or the frosting will become too soft, making it difficult to spread over the cupcakes.

Tiramisu Cake Pops makes 36 cake pops

Plain cupcake batter (page 26) 1 portion

Coffee powder 2 tsp

Coffee liqueur 3 Tbsp

Light brown sugar 45 g (1 1/2 oz)

Mascarpone cheese 250 g (9 oz)

Icing (confectioner's) sugar 45 g (1 1/2 oz), sifted

Vanilla extract 1 tsp

MASCARPONE CHEESE FILLING

Mascarpone cheese 500 g (1 lb 1 1/2 oz)

Icing (confectioner's) sugar 90 g (3 1/5 oz), sifted

Heavy cream 250 g (9 oz)

GARNISHING

Cocoa powder

Oreo sticks or cookies (optional)

1. Following the recipe for plain cupcakes, pour the batter into a 20-cm (8-in) round cake tin lined with parchment paper. Bake for 35–40 minutes or until light golden brown and dry to the touch. Remove from oven and leave to cool for 10 minutes, then remove from cake tin and place on a wire rack to cool completely.
2. Prepare coffee mixture. Combine coffee powder, coffee liqueur and brown sugar in a small bowl and mix well. Set aside.
3. Prepare mascarpone mixture. In a separate bowl, combine mascarpone cheese, icing sugar and vanilla extract. Mix well using a spatula.
4. Combine coffee mixture with mascarpone mixture. Stir thoroughly until it thickens to a smooth creamy consistency.
5. Cut cake into large pieces and using your hands, crumble them into a large mixing bowl.
6. Pour mixture prepared in step 4 into crumbled cake. Use a cake mixer to blend or you can use your hands. The resultant cake mixture should be crumbly.
7. Roll cake mixture into balls, each no bigger than 2.5 cm (1 in) in diameter. Place on a baking sheet lined with parchment paper. You should get 36 or more cake pops.
8. Refrigerate for at least 2 hours.

MASCARPONE CHEESE FILLING

9. Meanwhile, prepare mascarpone cheese filling. Using a spatula, combine mascarpone cheese and icing sugar in a bowl and mix well.
10. In a chilled bowl, whisk heavy cream using an electric mixer on high speed until stiff peaks form. Fold into mascarpone cheese.

ASSEMBLY

11. Spoon some mascarpone cheese filling into serving glasses. Dust with cocoa powder and place cake pops on top. Dust cocoa powder over again. Repeat if you prefer more layers. Finish by dusting over cocoa powder.
12. Serve with Oreo sticks or cookies if desired.

Italian goes pop! I am giving this favourite dessert a new spin, rolling them into cake pops and serving them in glasses. Fancy and always yummy!

Soft drink addicts will love these cupcakes! The addition of marshmallows makes them especially soft and fluffy. Serve them at parties and during the holidays, or whenever you want a treat! Add some drama and use bright red cupcake liners with maraschino cherries. Want more attitude? Frost the cupcakes with rum-spiked Coca-Cola buttercream!

Coca-Cola Cupcakes makes 12 cupcakes

Plain (all-purpose) flour 150 g (5 1/3 oz)

Baking soda 1/2 tsp

Caster sugar 200 g (7 oz)

Unsalted butter 65 g (2 1/3 oz)

Vegetable oil 4 Tbsp

Cocoa powder 1 1/2 Tbsp

Coca-Cola 125 ml (4 fl oz / 1/2 cup)

Small marshmallows 3/4 cup

Egg 1, lightly beaten

Buttermilk (page 20) 4 Tbsp

Vanilla extract 1 tsp

TOPPING

Coca Cola buttercream (page 154) *or* **rum-spiked Coca–Cola buttercream** (page 154)

Maraschino cherries

1. Preheat oven to 180°C (350°). Line muffin tray with cupcake liners.
2. Sift flour and baking soda into a bowl. Mix in sugar and set aside.
3. Combine butter, oil, cocoa powder and Coca-Cola in a saucepan and bring to a slow boil, stirring continuously until well blended. Allow to simmer and mix in marshmallows until they have dissolved. Pour onto dry ingredients prepared in step 2. Using a hand-held whisk, stir until well combined.
4. Add egg and whisk until well combined.
5. Add buttermilk and vanilla extract. Whisk until everything is well incorporated. Batter should be thick but of a pouring consistency.
6. Pour batter into cupcake liners until two-thirds full. Bake for 20–25 minutes or until a toothpick inserted into the centre of the cake comes out clean.
7. Remove from oven and let cupcakes sit in muffin tray for 10 minutes.
8. Remove cupcakes from tray and place on a wire rack to cool completely before frosting.
9. Top with twirls of Coca–Cola buttercream. Garnish with maraschino cherries, secured with toothpicks over the buttercream. Enjoy with a tall glass of iced Coca–Cola!

Note

- Transfer the batter into a pouring cup before filling the cupcake liners. This way, you avoid messy drips.
- I prefer to measure marshmallows by volume rather than by weight. Because they are so fluffy, volume measurements tend to be more accurate than weight measurements.

Ham and Cheese Cupcakes makes 12–15 cupcakes

Plain (all-purpose) flour 250 g (9 oz)

Baking powder 1 Tbsp

Salt $\frac{1}{2}$ tsp

Egg 1, lightly beaten

Buttermilk (page 21) 250 ml (8 fl oz / 1 cup)

Vegetable oil 50 ml ($1\frac{2}{3}$ fl oz)

Onions 50 g ($1\frac{2}{3}$ oz), peeled and chopped

Chunky ham 200 g (7 oz), chopped

Cheddar cheese 300 g ($10\frac{1}{2}$ oz), grated

TOPPING

Sour cream *or* **cream cheese frosting** (page 149)

chopped spring onions (scallions)

1. Preheat oven to 200°C (400°F). Grease muffin tray with a bit of butter or baking spray.
2. Whisk flour, baking powder and salt in a big bowl.
3. In a separate bowl, whisk egg, buttermilk and oil.
4. Add buttermilk mixture to dry ingredients prepared in step 2. Mix well.
5. With a spatula, fold in onions, ham and cheese.
6. Spoon batter into muffin tray until three-quarters full. Bake for 20 minutes or until cupcakes are golden brown on top.
7. Remove from the oven and let cupcakes sit in muffin tray for 10 minutes.
8. Remove cupcakes from tray and place on a wire rack to cool completely before frosting.
9. Serve with sour cream and spring onion dip. Alternatively, spread a layer of cream cheese frosting over cupcakes and top with spring onions.

For friends and family who love cheese, this is a godsend. My mother, who has excluded cheese from her diet for years, cannot resist these cupcakes. The texture is more muffin-like, but thoroughly savoury because of the ham and cheese. Use canned luncheon meat or SPAM if you don't have ham on hand. Eat as a dessert or as a side to a main meal. Breakfast with these babies will be memorable too.

Chocolate Chip Cake Pops makes 36–40 cake pops

Plain cupcake batter
(page 26) 1 portion

Vanilla buttercream
(page 154) 200 g (7 oz)

Mini chocolate chips or **chocolate pearls** 100 g (3$\frac{1}{2}$ oz)

Semi-sweet chocolate couverture 200 g (7 oz)

Vegetable shortening (optional) 1 Tbsp

Lollipop sticks 30–40

1. Following the recipe for plain cupcakes, pour the batter into a 20-cm (8-in) round cake tin lined with parchment paper. Bake for 35–40 minutes or until light golden brown and dry to the touch. Remove from oven and leave to cool for 10 minutes, then remove from cake tin and place on a wire rack to cool completely.
2. Cut cake into large pieces and crumble into a big bowl.
3. Add half of the vanilla buttercream to crumbled cake. Use a cake mixer to blend or you can use your hands. Add remainder of buttercream and continue blending. Ensure that mixture is not too wet or mushy. The resultant cake mixture should be crumbly.
4. Fold in the mini chocolate chips or chocolate pearls.
5. Roll cake mixture into balls, each no bigger than 2.5 cm (1 in) in diameter. Place them on a baking sheet lined with parchment paper. Chill in the refrigerator for at least 2 hours.
6. When the cake balls are well chilled, prepare chocolate. Melt chocolate couverture in a double boiler or bain-marie. Once melted, add vegetable shortening and mix well.
7. Dip ends of lollipop sticks into melted chocolate. Using the chocolate-coated end, pierce each cake ball at least half way through—be gentle, lest the cake balls crack. Return cake pops into the refrigerator for another 15 minutes for the chocolate-coated lollipop sticks to adhere to the cake balls.
8. Remove melted chocolate from heat and allow to cool for awhile.
9. Hold on to lollipop stick and roll cake ball in melted chocolate. Repeat for remaining cake balls.
10. Stand cake pops in tall glasses and let the chocolate set before serving.

These are easy to make albeit more time-consuming than cupcakes. Children (and even adults!) simply love these cake pops.

Irresistibly Smooth

luscious flavours that put you in the mood

the saint	58
red head	60
white choco cherry cupcakes	62
strawberry cupcakes	64
pistachio-raspberry delight	67
almond orange cupcakes	68
pecan caramel cupcakes	71
red velvet redefined	72

The Saint *makes 15 cupcakes*

Egg whites from 3 eggs
Full cream milk 150 ml (5 fl oz)
Vanilla extract 1 tsp
Plain (all-purpose) flour 200 g (7 oz)
Caster sugar 200 g (7 oz)
Baking powder 1 tsp
Salt a pinch
Unsalted butter 125 g (4½ oz)

TOPPING
White chocolate gananche (page 148) *or* **your choice of buttercream** (pages 152–156)

1. Preheat oven to 180°C (350°F). Line muffin tray with cupcake liners.
2. Whisk egg whites, 3 Tbsp milk and vanilla extract in a bowl.
3. In a separate mixing bowl, combine flour, sugar, baking powder and salt. Mix well.
4. Add butter and remaining milk. Beat in electric mixer on low speed until well incorporated. Do not over beat.
5. Increase the speed of the mixer and gradually add egg white mixture prepared in step 2. Ensure it is well incorporated. The resultant batter should be smooth.
6. Pour batter into cupcake liners until three-quarters full. Bake for 20–25 minutes. Remove from oven and let cupcakes sit in muffin tray for 5 minutes.
7. Remove cupcakes from tray and place on a wire rack to cool completely before frosting.
8. Top with white chocolate ganache or your choice of buttercream frosting before serving.

Note

- Get creative and add fresh or preserved fruits of your choice! Consider folding 50 g (1⅔ oz) chopped dried apricots into the batter before baking. Top cupcakes with a slather of apricot jam.

This is a heavenly recipe that produces a smooth and velvety white cake that is easy to make and classy on its own. Perfect with any white frosting or fruity buttercream of your choice.

Red Head makes 12 cupcakes

Plain (all-purpose) flour 165 g (5$^2/_3$ oz), sifted

Cocoa powder 1 Tbsp, sifted

Baking soda $^1/_2$ tsp

Baking powder $^1/_2$ tsp

Salt a pinch

Buttermilk (Page 20) 250 ml (8 fl oz / 1 cup)

Red food colouring 1 tsp

Vanilla extract 1 tsp

Caster sugar 130 g (4$^2/_3$ oz)

Unsalted butter 60 g (2 oz), softened

Egg whites from 2 eggs

TOPPING

Cream cheese frosting (page 149)

Desiccated coconut (optional)

or **raspberry buttercream** (page 154)

1. Preheat oven to 180°C (350°F). Line muffin tray with cupcake liners.
2. Whisk flour, cocoa powder, baking soda, baking powder and salt in a bowl. Set aside.
3. Combine buttermilk, food colouring and vanilla extract in a separate bowl. Stir to mix.
4. Beat sugar and butter in an electric mixer at medium speed for about 5 minutes. Gradually add egg whites and continue to beat at medium speed for 5 minutes or until mixture is light and fluffy.
5. Add flour mixture prepared in step 2, alternating with buttermilk mixture prepared in step 3. Begin and end with flour mixture. Continue to beat until well incorporated.
6. Pour batter into cupcake liners until three-quarters full. Bake for 25 minutes or until a toothpick inserted into the centre of cakes comes out clean. Remove from oven and let cupcakes sit in tray for 5 minutes.
7. Remove cupcakes from tray and place on a wire rack to cool completely before frosting.
8. Pipe a thick layer of cream cheese frosting on top. Sprinkle a generous amount of desiccated coconut over the cream cheese if you like. Alternatively, spread raspberry buttercream on top of cupcakes.

A salute to America's favourite red velvet cake! For those who like their cupcakes really red, use a strawberry-red food colouring and double the suggested amount here. For those who prefer to use natural colouring, a small amount of beetroot juice can be used in place of food colouring.

White Choco Cherry Cupcakes *makes 15 cupcakes*

Unsalted butter 125 g (4½ oz)

White chocolate couverture 80 g (2⅘ oz)

Caster sugar 125 g (4½ oz)

Eggs 2, lightly beaten

Salt a pinch

Self-raising flour 125 g (4½ oz)

Morello cherry jam 150 g (5⅓ oz)

TOPPING

Cream cheese frosting (page 149)

White chocolate curls *or* **shavings**

Fresh cherries

1. Preheat oven to 180°C (350°F). Line muffin tray with cupcake liners.
2. Melt butter in a heavy-bottomed pan over low to medium heat. Stir butter using a hand-held whisk. Avoid burning the butter.
3. When butter is completely melted, remove from heat immediately and stir in white chocolate. Whisk butter and white chocolate together until fully incorporated and smooth. Mixture may be lumpy but that is fine.
4. Add sugar and continue stirring until sugar has dissolved.
5. Gradually add eggs and continue to whisk.
6. Add salt and flour. Stir until well mixed.
7. Gently stir in jam, making sure not to over mix.
8. Spoon batter into cupcake liners until half to two-thirds full. Bake for 20–25 minutes, or until cupcakes have risen and are light golden brown in colour. Remove from oven and let cupcakes sit in muffin tray for 10 minutes.
9. Remove cupcakes from tray and place on a wire rack to cool completely before frosting.
10. Spread a thick layer of cream cheese frosting on top of cupcakes and sprinkle with white chocolate curls or shavings. Top with fresh cherries.

Note

- If you prefer it less sweet, you may reduce the amount of sugar in the cupcakes to 100 g (3½ oz).
- You may wish to bake this as a cake. This same recipe can be baked using a 20-cm (8-in) round tin lined with parchment paper. Bake for 40–45 minutes. Test doneness with a toothpick inserted into the centre of the cake—the toothpick should come out clean.

I created this indulgently rich cupcake that uses white chocolate and morello cherry jam. This makes a wonderful after-dinner treat, and your guests will be bowled over! The sweetness of the cupcakes is well balanced with the slightly tart cream cheese.

Strawberry Cupcakes *makes 12 cupcakes*

Plain (all-purpose) flour 165 g (5^2/$_3$ oz), sifted

Baking powder 1 tsp

Coarse salt ^{1}/$_4$ tsp

Fresh or frozen strawberries 100 g (3^1/$_2$ oz), thawed if frozen

Full cream milk 4 Tbsp

Vanilla extract 1 tsp

Unsalted butter 125 g (4^1/$_2$ oz)

Sugar 200 g (7 oz)

Egg 1, large, lightly beaten

Egg whites from 2 large eggs

TOPPING

Strawberry buttercream (page 155)

Fresh strawberry slices

1. Preheat oven to 180°C (350°F). Line muffin tray with cupcake liners.
2. In a bowl, sift flour, baking powder and salt together. Set aside.
3. Process strawberries in a blender to get about 100 g (3^1/$_2$ oz) of strawberry purée. (Any extra puree should be saved for making strawberry buttercream.)
4. Combine milk, vanilla extract and strawberry purée in a small bowl. Set aside.
5. Cream butter in an electric mixer for a few minutes. Gradually add sugar and continue to beat until well combined.
6. Add egg and egg whites. Beat until well blended.
7. Add half the flour mixture prepared in step 2, followed by the strawberry mixture prepared in step 4. Continue beating. Add the remaining flour mixture and continue to beat until batter is well mixed.
8. Spoon batter into cupcake liners until three-quarters full. Bake for 20–25 minutes. Remove from oven and let cupcakes sit in muffin tray for 5 minutes.
9. Remove cupcakes from tray and place on a wire rack to cool completely before frosting.
10. Pipe strawberry buttercream on top of cupcakes and top with slices of fresh strawberries.

Note

- Consider using cake flour in place of plain flour to get fluffier cupcakes.
- Fold bits of strawberries into the cake batter to give the cupcakes added crunch and fruitiness.
- You can turn this cupcake into a wicked dessert!
  1. In a bowl, mix 100 ml (3^1/$_2$ oz) champagne with 50 ml (1^2/$_3$ fl oz) brandy.
  2. Soak the bits and chucks of strawberries overnight (or at least for a few hours). Drain the strawberries before folding them into the batter.
  3. If there's leftover champagne and brandy, add them to the strawberry buttercream.

For the health freaks in all of us, use organic strawberries and if you can, reduce sugar by 25–50 g (1–1²⁄₃ oz). To make this cake really stand out, choose really red strawberries. By the way, the strawberry buttercream tastes like ice cream!

To the Chinese, pistachios symbolise happiness. Enjoy this during any festive occasion, or simply as an afternoon tea favourite!

Pistachio-Raspberry Delight makes 12 cupcakes

Unsalted pistachios 150 g (5$\frac{1}{3}$ oz), shelled and whole + 35 g (1$\frac{1}{4}$ oz), shelled and roughly chopped

Caster sugar 300 g (10$\frac{1}{2}$ oz)

Salt 1 tsp

Unsalted butter 125 g (4$\frac{1}{2}$ oz)

Vanilla extract 2 tsp

Eggs 4

Plain (all-purpose) flour 150 g (5$\frac{1}{3}$ oz)

Fresh or frozen raspberries 150 g (5$\frac{1}{3}$ oz)

TOPPING

Icing (confectioner's) sugar *or* **cream cheese frosting** (page 149)

Raspberries *or* **cranberries**

1. Preheat oven to 180°C (350°F). Line muffin tray with cupcake liners.
2. In a blender, finely grind pistachios with sugar and salt.
3. Beat butter, vanilla extract and eggs with an electric mixer until smooth.
4. Add ground pistachios and flour a little at a time. Mix well until ingredients are incorporated.
5. Spoon batter into cupcake liners until three-quarters full.
6. Drop 3–4 raspberries into batter and sprinkle chopped pistachios over.
7. Bake for 25–30 minutes or until golden brown. Remove from oven and let cupcakes sit in muffin tray for 5 minutes.
8. Remove cupcakes from tray and place on a wire rack to cool.
9. Serve these delightful cupcakes warm or cooled. Sift icing sugar over before serving. For an indulgent treat, spread a thick layer of cream cheese frosting on top of cupcakes and top with raspberries or cranberries.

Note

- You may use dried cranberries in place of fresh or frozen raspberries. Gently fold 120 g (4$\frac{1}{3}$ oz) dried cranberries into the batter by drawing a figure 8 several times. Sift 1 Tbsp flour over dried cranberries before dropping them into the batter so they don't sink to the bottom during baking.

Almond Orange Cupcakes *makes 15 cupcakes*

Whole oranges 2

Unsalted butter 175 g (6¼ oz)

Caster sugar 175 g (6¼ oz)

Eggs 3, lightly beaten

Plain (all-purpose) flour 150 g (5⅓ oz)

Almond meal 30 g (1 oz)

Almond essence 1 tsp

Full cream milk (optional) 2 Tbsp

TOPPING

White chocolate buttercream (page 154) or **vanilla buttercream** (page 154)

1. Wash oranges. Leave the peel on. In a heavy-bottomed saucepan, cover whole oranges with water and bring to the boil. Reduce heat and simmer for 30 minutes or until oranges are soft.
2. Allow oranges to cool a little. Cut the oranges into large pieces and remove the seeds. Blend oranges until smooth. Set aside 150 g (5⅓ oz) puréed orange to use for cupcakes. Allow to cool before use.
3. Preheat oven to 180°C (350°F). Line muffin tray with cupcake liners.
4. Cream butter in an electric mixer for a few minutes. Gradually add sugar and continue to beat until well combined.
5. Add eggs and beat until mixture is well blended, light and fluffy.
6. Add flour, almond meal and almond essence. Continue to beat on medium speed until well mixed. Stop immediately once everything is well combined. Fold in the puréed orange using a spatula. Add milk if using and mix well.
7. Spoon batter into cupcake liners until three-quarters full. Bake for 25–30 minutes or until cupcakes are slightly golden brown and a toothpick inserted into the centre of the cakes comes out clean.
8. Remove from oven and let cupcakes sit in muffin tray for 10 minutes.
9. Remove cupcakes from tray and place on a wire rack to cool completely before frosting.
10. Top with white chocolate buttercream or vanilla buttercream.

Note

- To bake cupcakes with a lighter and softer texture, use cake flour in place of plain flour.
- Should you want to bake a full cake, this will be a wonderful recipe to try. Line a 20-cm (8-in) square tin or 22.5-cm (9-in) round tin with parchment paper. Following the recipe above, pour batter into cake tin and pop it into the oven for at least 45 minutes. To test doneness, insert a toothpick into the centre of the cake, which should come out clean when the cake is ready.

These cupcakes have a dense and moist texture. The sweetness of almond is encompassed in the tartness of orange. When combined with luxurious white chocolate buttercream, it's rich without being overpowering. A notable DJ who ordered this as a birthday cake said it goes fabulously well with champagne!

I must confess that I simply love caramel and its frosting, and I am guilty of making these pecan cupcakes that go wonderfully well with it!

Pecan Caramel Cupcakes *makes 12 cupcakes*

Self-raising flour 125 g (4$^{1}/_{2}$ oz)

Cocoa powder 2 Tbsp

Unsalted butter 125 g (4$^{1}/_{2}$ oz)

Caster sugar 125 (4$^{1}/_{2}$ oz)

Eggs 2, lightly beaten

Vanilla extract 1 tsp

Chopped pecans 60 g (2 oz)

TOPPING

Sea salt caramel frosting (page 166)

Pecans

Salt crystals (optional)

1. Preheat oven to 180°C (350°F). Line muffin tray with cupcake liners.
2. Sift flour and cocoa powder together into a bowl. Set aside.
3. Cream butter in an electric mixer for a few minutes. Gradually add sugar and continue to beat until well combined.
4. Add eggs and beat until mixture is well blended, light and fluffy.
5. Add vanilla extract and mix well.
6. Add flour and cocoa mixture prepared in step 2, and continue to beat until well mixed. Stop immediately once all the flour has mixed well into the batter. Using a spatula, fold in pecans.
7. Spoon batter into the cupcake liners until three-quarters full. Bake for 20–25 minutes. Remove from oven and let cupcakes sit in muffin tray for 5 minutes.
8. Remove cupcakes from the tray and place on a wire rack to cool completely before frosting.
9. Garnish with a generous layer of sea salt caramel frosting over cupcakes. Top with pecans. Sprinkle some salt crystals over the frosting if desired.

Note
- For more chocolaty cupcakes, add up to 3 Tbsp cocoa powder to the batter.
- Keep pecans fresh in the refrigerator. Pecans not kept in a chilled environment tend to oxidise easily and may develop an odour.

Red Velvet Redefined makes 45–50 cake pops

Red head cake batter
(page 60) 1 portion

Vanilla buttercream (page 154)
300 g (10½ oz)

Mini marshmallows (optional)

White chocolate couverture
200 g (7 oz)

Raspberry sorbet (optional)

1. Following the recipe for red head cupcakes, pour batter into a 20-cm (8-in) round cake tin lined with parchment paper. Bake for 45–50 minutes or until cake is dry to the touch. A toothpick inserted into the centre of the cake should come out clean. If not, pop the cake back into the oven and bake for another 5–10 minutes. Remove from oven and leave to cool for 10 minutes, then remove from cake tin and place on a wire rack to cool completely.

2. Cut the cake into big pieces and crumble into a big bowl. (The outer area of the cake could be hard but this is fine.)

3. Add half the vanilla buttercream into crumbled cake. Use a cake mixer to blend or you can use your hands. Add remaining buttercream bit by bit and continue to blend. Ensure that mixture is not too wet or mushy from the buttercream. The resultant cake mixture should be crumbly.

4. Flatten some cake mixture in your hand. Place a mini marshmallow, if using, onto flattened cake and roll into a ball of no more than 2.5 cm (1 in) in diameter. Make sure the marshmallow is in the centre. Place cake balls on a baking sheet lined with parchment paper and chill in the refrigerator for at least 2 hours.

5. Meanwhile, melt white chocolate couverture in a double boiler or bain-marie. Once melted, remove from heat. Leave to cool for 5 minutes before using.

6. Take cake balls out of the refrigerator and dip into melted chocolate, using 2 teaspoons to help you. Return cake pops to the baking sheet and refrigerate until chocolate sets.

7. Serve with raspberry sorbet if desired.

Note

- If the cake mixture is too dry after step 3, add 1 Tbsp or more milk as needed. If too wet, add 3–4 Tbsp sifted icing sugar.

Red velvet cake is always a welcome treat, but red velvet cake pops bring this cake to a new level. The marshmallow centre makes this a pleasant surprise for all!

delicious, guilt-free indulgence for the health-conscious

dairy-free cupcakes	76
hot and puffed cupcakes	78
kiwi vegan cupcakes	80
gluten-free orange cupcakes	82
wolfberry chocolaty prune cupcakes	85
eat your vegetables	86
lemon berry	88
sweet potato cranberry cupcakes	91

Dairy-free Cupcakes makes 12 cupcakes

Self-raising flour 175 g (6¼ oz)

Baking powder ½ tsp

Caster sugar 75 g (2⅔ oz)

Unsweetened soy milk 150 ml (5 fl oz)

Egg 1

Vegetable oil 2 Tbsp

Vanilla extract (optional) 1 tsp

Salt (optional) a pinch

1. Preheat oven to 200°C (400°F). Line muffin tray with cupcake liners.
2. Sift flour and baking powder together into a bowl. Stir in sugar with a hand-held whisk.
3. In a separate bowl, whisk soy milk, egg and oil to form a light mixture. Pour into flour mixture prepared in step 2.
4. Stir lightly and once well mixed, stop stirring or the cupcakes will be tough.
5. Add vanilla extract and salt if using. Mix lightly.
6. Spoon mixture into cupcake liners until three-quarters full. Bake for about 15 minutes. Remove from oven and let cupcakes sit in muffin tray for 5 minutes.
7. Remove cupcakes from tray and place on a wire rack to cool before serving or frosting.
8. Frost cupcakes if desired.

This is a great cupcake recipe for lacto-vegetarians.

Hot and Puffed Cupcakes makes 18 cupcakes

Self-raising flour 60 g (2 oz)

Cornflour (cornstarch) 60 g (2 oz)

Ground ginger 3 tsp

Ground cinnamon 1 tsp

Ground nutmeg ½ tsp

Cocoa powder 3 tsp

Eggs 5, yolks and whites separated

Caster sugar 125 g (4½ oz)

Golden syrup 1 Tbsp

Whipped topping cream (page 159)

Store-bought apple sauce

1. Preheat oven to 190°C (375°F). Line muffin tray with cupcake liners.
2. Sift flour, cornflour, spices and cocoa powder together several times. I suggest sifting three to five times.
3. Beat egg whites in an electric mixer on high until soft peaks form. Continue beating and add sugar a little at a time. Ensure each portion of sugar has dissolved before adding more.
4. Add egg yolks and golden syrup. Continue to beat until mixture is well combined.
5. Using a spatula, fold flour mixture prepared in step 2 into batter until well combined.
6. Spoon batter into cupcake liners until three-quarters full. Bake for 15–20 minutes until cupcakes are dark brown with a dry texture. Remove from oven and let cupcakes sit in muffin tray for 5 minutes.
7. Remove cupcakes from tray and place on a wire rack to cool completely.
8. Serve cupcakes as they are with whipped topping cream and apple sauce on the side.

Note

- For a stronger ginger and spice flavour, omit the cocoa powder and replace with an equal amount of self-raising flour.

These cupcakes are dedicated to my two friends, John and Theresa, the eternal gym enthusiasts! Appropriately named Hot and Puffed, these airy sponge-like cupcakes are out of this world, as Theresa coos. Ginger makes the cupcakes hot, and sifting the flours makes them light. No butter is used so the recipe is figure-friendly. Of course, the eggs give John and Theresa their much needed protein intake.

Kiwi Vegan Cupcakes makes 12 cupcakes

Plain (all-purpose) flour 265 g (9$^1/_2$ oz)

Baking soda 1 tsp

Caster sugar 165 g (5$^4/_5$ oz)

Olive or vegetable oil 125 ml (4 fl oz / $^1/_2$ cup)

White vinegar 1 Tbsp

Vanilla extract 1 tsp

Puréed kiwi 225 g (8 oz)

TOPPING

Icing (confectioner's) sugar *or* **kiwi glaze** (page 163)

1. Preheat oven to 185°C (365°F). Line muffin tray with cupcake liners.
2. Whisk flour, baking soda and sugar in a bowl.
3. In another bowl, combine oil, vinegar and vanilla extract. Add puréed kiwi. Ensure all ingredients are well incorporated. Slowly add to flour mixture. Using a cake mixer, gently whisk until all ingredients are well combined.
4. Spoon batter into cupcake liners until three-quarters full. Bake for 30–35 minutes. The cupcakes should be dry to touch or a little crusty on top. Test doneness with a toothpick inserted into the centre of cakes. The toothpick should come out clean. Remove from oven and let cupcakes sit in muffin tray for 5 minutes.
5. Remove cupcakes from tray and place on a wire rack to cool completely before frosting.
6. Dust some icing sugar over cupcakes before serving. Alternatively, spoon kiwi glaze over cupcakes.

Note

- Choose almost-ripe kiwi fruit. You may also add some kiwi chunks—that way, there will be some bits of fruits when you bite into the cupcakes.
- Using cake flour in place of plain flour gives a lighter and softer texture. Baking times can be shortened to 25–30 minutes. Always test doneness with a toothpick inserted into the centre of the cake, and the toothpick should come out clean.

Kiwi fruit is rich in antioxidants such as vitamins C and E, is a good source of folic acid and potassium, and helps improve our immune systems. I also read that kiwi fruit helps reduce the risk of cardiovascular diseases. So go on, have cupcakes for better health! These cupcakes are made without eggs and butter. You may substitute kiwi fruit in this recipe with strawberries or mild-flavoured fruits like peaches or dragon fruits.

Gluten-free Orange Cupcakes <small>makes 12 cupcakes</small>

Whole oranges 2
Almond meal 100 g (3½ oz)
Baking soda 1½ tsp
Unsalted butter 65 g (2⅓ oz)
Caster sugar 165 g (5⅘ oz)
Eggs 3

TOPPING
White chocolate ganache (page 148) *or* **white chocolate buttercream** (page 154)
Orange slices

1. Wash oranges. Leave the peel on. In a heavy-based saucepan, cover whole oranges with water and bring to a boil. Turn down the heat and simmer for about 1 hour or until oranges are very soft. Set aside to cool.

2. Cut the oranges into big pieces and remove seeds. Blend until smooth. Set aside 150 g (5⅓ oz) puréed orange.

3. Preheat oven to 180°C (350°F). Line muffin tray with cupcake liners.

4. Whisk almond meal and baking soda in a small bowl. Set aside.

5. Cream butter in an electric mixer for a few minutes. Gradually add sugar and continue to beat until well combined.

6. Add eggs and beat until mixture is well blended, light and fluffy.

7. Add half the almond meal mixture prepared in step 4 and beat on low speed until well combined. Add orange purée and beat until well mixed. Add remaining almond meal and mix until fully incorporated.

8. Spoon batter into cupcake liners until three-quarters full. Bake for 30 minutes or until cupcakes look dry and slightly brown. Remove from the oven and let cupcakes sit in muffin tray for 5 minutes.

9. Remove from tray and place on a wire rack to cool completely before frosting.

10. Top with white chocolate ganache or white chocolate buttercream. Garnish with orange slices.

Gluten-free cupcakes can be dry, but I have used almond meal in this flour-less recipe, and thanks to the fresh oranges, these cupcakes are moist. They taste speechlessly delicious with white chocolate ganache or buttercream!

I baked these cupcakes as a birthday surprise for my American friend, Frances, who is over 65 years old and fit as a fiddle! I used Frances' favourite fruit, wolfberries (also commonly known as goji berries), in these cupcakes. Wolfberries are good for our eyes and contain lots of vitamins and minerals. I used prunes here, so no butter and sugar are needed. Combined with chocolate, they make healthy snacks suitable for everyone!

Wolfberry Chocolaty Prune Cupcakes
makes 12 cupcakes

Prunes 250 g (9 oz), pitted

Boiling water 400 ml (13$\frac{1}{2}$ fl oz)

Dried Chinese wolfberries 50 g (1$\frac{2}{3}$ oz)

Semi-sweet chocolate couverture 60 g (2 oz), melted

Vanilla extract 1 tsp

Self-raising flour 100 g (3$\frac{1}{2}$ oz)

Egg whites from 2 eggs

TOPPING

Blanched wolfberries

Icing (confectioner's) sugar (optional)

1. Cover and soak prunes in 300 ml (10 fl oz / 1$\frac{1}{4}$ cups) boiling water for at least 30 minutes. Purée prunes in a blender and set aside.
2. Pour remaining boiling water over dried wolfberries. Soak for 3 minutes—they should be soft, not mushy. Drain and set aside.
3. Melt chocolate couverture in a bowl set over a pot of boiling water. Stir with a wooden spoon until chocolate has melted. Remove from heat and allow to cool before using.
4. Preheat oven to 180°C (350°F). Line muffin tray with cupcake liners.
5. Prepare cake mixture. Combine prune purée, vanilla extract, flour and half the wolfberries in a bowl. Mix well. Add melted chocolate and stir to mix.
6. Beat egg whites in an electric mixer with a whisk attachment until stiff peaks form. Using a spatula, fold egg whites into cake mixture until well combined.
7. Spoon batter into cupcake liners until three-quarters full. Bake for 20–25 minutes. Remove from oven and let cupcakes sit in muffin tray for 5 minutes.
8. Remove cupcakes from tray and place on a wire rack to cool completely.
9. Top with remaining wolfberries. Dust some icing sugar over cupcakes if desired.

Eat Your Vegetables makes 12 cupcakes

Plain (all-purpose) flour
225 g (8 oz)

Baking soda 1/2 tsp

Ground cinnamon 1 1/2 tsp

Ground clove 1/2 tsp

Salt 1/2 tsp

Vegetable oil 150 ml (5 fl oz)

Sugar 200 g (7 oz)

Vanilla extract 1 tsp

Eggs 2

Soy milk (unsweetened)
4 Tbsp

Shredded carrots 220 g (7 4/5 oz)

Frozen peas 80 g (2 4/5 oz)

TOPPING

Plain yoghurt

1. Preheat oven to 180°C (350°F). Line muffin tray with cupcake liners.
2. Sift flour, baking soda, cinnamon, clove and salt into a bowl. Set aside.
3. Combine oil and sugar in a mixing bowl and beat on medium speed. Add vanilla extract and mix well.
4. Add eggs and continue beating until well combined.
5. Add soy milk and half the flour mixture prepared in step 2. Mix well before adding the remaining flour mixture. Stop immediately once all the flour has been mixed well into the batter.
6. Fold in shredded carrots and peas with a spatula.
7. Spoon batter into cupcake liners until three-quarters full. Bake for 20–25 minutes.
8. Remove from the oven and leave cupcakes in the muffin tray for 5 minutes.
9. Remove cupcakes from tray and place on a wire rack to cool completely before serving.
10. Top cupcakes with a spoonful of plain yoghurt.

Note

- For a more savoury experience, increase amount of salt to 1 tsp.
- You may use cake flour here for a lighter texture.
- For an even healthier option, replace a portion (or all) of the plain flour with wholemeal flour. The texture will be harder, so you will need to increase the amount of soy milk up to 90 ml (3 fl oz / 3/8 cup).

I came up with these carrot and pea cupcakes at the spur of the moment, grabbing whatever I had in the fridge. I was desperate to get the kids to eat their vegetables! The cupcakes use neither butter nor cow's milk, and are perfect for the lactose-intolerant. These are great at any time of the day and they taste surprisingly good! They are wonderfully nutritious when served with plain yoghurt.

Lemon Berry makes 12 cupcakes

Plain (all-purpose) flour 200 g (7 oz)

Baking powder 1½ tsp

Baking soda ½ tsp

Sugar 150 g (5 oz)

Salt ¼ tsp

Unsalted butter 65 g (2⅓ oz), melted

Egg 1, lightly beaten

Buttermilk (page 20) 125 ml (4 fl oz / ½ cup)

Full cream milk 125 ml (4 fl oz / ½ cup)

Vanilla extract 1 tsp

Lemon rind grated from ½ lemon

Lemon essential oil 5 drops

Fresh raspberries 12

Fresh blueberries 12

Fresh blackberries 12

TOPPING

Whipped topping cream (page 159)

Fresh raspberries

Fresh blueberries

Fresh blackberries

1. Preheat oven to 180°C (350°F). Line muffin tray with cupcake liners.
2. Sift flour, baking powder and baking soda into a bowl. Mix sugar and salt into the flour mixture. Set aside.
3. Prepare buttermilk mixture. Combine butter and egg in a bowl. Stir with a whisk. Add buttermilk, milk, vanilla extract, lemon rind and lemon essential oil. Continue to whisk until everything is well incorporated.
4. Slowly add buttermilk mixture into flour mixture prepared in step 2. Whisk until batter is well blended and moist.
5. Spoon batter into cupcake liners until two-thirds full. Drop 1 raspberry, 1 blueberry and 1 blackberry into each cupcake liner.
6. Bake for 20–25 minutes. Remove from oven and let cupcakes sit in muffin tray for 5 minutes.
7. Remove cupcakes from tray and place on a wire rack to cool completely before frosting.
8. Using the back of a spoon, spread whipped topping cream over cupcakes. Top with raspberries, blueberries and blackberries.

This is the ever popular lemon-scented cupcakes, but made really special with the use of mixed berries. The cupcakes have a soft and delicate texture, and the juicy berries simply explode in your mouth with every bite! Dedicated to my good friend, Sius, who believes in eating and living well.

I exercise regularly to stay fit and believe in eating right, but nonetheless, I still need my cupcake fix! So, I have combined three of my favourite healthy foods here—sweet potato, cranberries and tofu—to give you this unusual but great tasting cupcake!

Sweet Potato Cranberry Cupcakes <small>makes 12 cupcakes</small>

Sweet potatoes 300 g (10½ oz)

Plain (all-purpose) flour 100 g (3½ oz) + 1 Tbsp for sifting over dried cranberries

Baking powder 1 tsp

Baking soda 1 tsp

Salt ½ tsp

Ground cinnamon 1 tsp

Ground ginger ½ tsp

Unsalted butter 125 g (4½ oz)

Sugar 100 g (3½ oz)

Eggs 2, lightly beaten

Soy milk (unsweetened) 2 Tbsp

Dried cranberries 100 g (3½ oz)

TOPPING

Tofu frosting (page 165)

Dried cranberries

1. Steam sweet potatoes. When done, remove the skin and mash. Set aside.
2. Preheat oven to 180°C (350°F). Line muffin tray with cupcake liners.
3. Whisk flour, baking powder, baking soda, salt, cinnamon and ginger into a bowl. Set aside.
4. Cream butter in an electric mixer for a few minutes. Gradually add sugar and continue to beat until well combined.
5. Add eggs and beat until mixture is well blended, light and fluffy.
6. Add flour mixture prepared in step 3. Continue to beat until well mixed. Stop immediately once all the flour has been mixed well into the batter.
7. Add mashed sweet potatoes and soy milk. Mix well.
8. Sift 1 Tbsp flour over cranberries. Using a spatula, fold cranberries into the batter.
9. Spoon batter into cupcake liners until two-thirds full. Bake for 20–25 minutes. Remove from oven and let cupcakes sit in muffin tray for 5 minutes.
10. Remove cupcakes from tray and place on a wire rack to cool completely before frosting.
11. Dip cupcakes into tofu frosting and top with cranberries. Alternatively, serve cupcakes as they are with tofu frosting on the side, garnished with cranberries.

Note

- The sweet potatoes are a treat by themselves already, so you may reduce the amount of sugar to 50 g (1⅔ oz) if desired.

Spicy Cool

cupcakes flavoured with spices and asian ingredients

go green cupcakes	94
apple cinnamon cupcakes	96
teh si cupcakes	99
milo cupcakes	100
horlicks cupcakes	102
kaya surprise cupcakes	104
spiced mocha madness	106
ginger bro cupcakes	108
yummy orange cardamom cupcakes	110
lemongrass cupcakes	113

Go Green Cupcakes makes 12 cupcakes

Self-raising flour 175 g
(6¼ oz)

Green tea powder 2 tsp

Salt a pinch

Caster sugar 125 g (4½ oz)

Vegetable oil 125 ml
(4½ fl oz / ½ cup)

Eggs 2, large

Vanilla extract 1 tsp

Full cream milk 4 Tbsp

Canned azuki beans 100 g
(3½ oz), drained

TOPPING

Mascarpone frosting
(page 150)

Green tea powder

Azuki beans (optional)

1. Preheat oven to 180°C (350°F). Line muffin tray with cupcake liners.
2. Sift flour, green tea powder and salt together in a bowl. Set aside.
3. Beat sugar, oil and eggs in an electric mixer until smooth. Add vanilla extract.
4. Gradually add flour mixture prepared in step 2, alternating with milk. Do not overbeat—stop immediately once everything has been well combined.
5. Gently fold in azuki beans using a spatula.
6. Spoon batter into cupcake liners until three-quarters full. Bake for 20–25 minutes or until a toothpick inserted into the centre of cakes comes out clean. Remove from oven and let cupcakes sit in muffin tray for 5 minutes.
7. Remove cupcakes from tray and place on a wire rack to cool completely before frosting.
8. Slather a thick layer of mascarpone frosting on top of cupcakes and dust over green tea powder. Serve with a dollop of azuki beans if desired.

Note

- Some canned azuki beans can be overly sweet. Reduce the amount of caster sugar to 100 g (3½ oz) if desired.

Green tea and azuki beans are staples of the Asian culinary experience. This perennial favourite pair is combined in a cupcake and made extra special with mascarpone frosting! Did I say that green tea is chock-full of antioxidants?

Apple Cinnamon Cupcakes makes 12 cupcakes

Unsalted butter 125 g (4½ oz)

Brown sugar 125 g (4½ oz)

Eggs 2, lightly beaten

Self-raising flour 125 g (4½ oz) + 1 Tbsp for sifting over apples

Ground cinnamon 2 tsp

Dessert apples 2, one of them cored and roughly chopped, the other cored and thinly sliced

GLAZE

Apricot glaze 3 Tbsp

Hot water 1½ Tbsp

1. Preheat oven to 180°C (350°F). Line muffin tray with cupcake liners.
2. Cream butter in an electric mixer for a few minutes. Gradually add brown sugar and continue to beat until well combined.
3. Add eggs and beat until mixture is well blended, light and fluffy.
4. Add flour and cinnamon. Continue to beat until well mixed. Stop immediately once all the flour has been mixed well into the batter.
5. Sift 1 Tbsp self-raising flour over apples. Using a spatula, fold chopped apples into batter.
6. Spoon batter into cupcake liners until three-quarters full. Arrange 2–3 apple slices on top. Bake for 20–25 minutes. Remove from oven and let cupcakes sit in muffin tray for 5 minutes.
7. Remove cupcakes from tray and place on a wire rack to cool.
8. Meanwhile, prepare glaze. Use a brush to mix apricot glaze with hot water until they combine and mixture is of spreadable consistency. While cupcakes are still warm, spread a thin layer of apricot glaze on top.

Note

- To prevent apples from browning, soak apples in lightly salted water for about 5 minutes and dry on paper napkins before using.
- No apricot glaze? No problem! Just use apricot jam—pass it through a sieve before mixing with hot water.

This is a healthy dessert that is enjoyed by both young and old. Use crunchy red apples for the best results. The sheen from the apricot glaze makes these cupcakes irresistibly appetising!

Teh si *is a popular drink in Singapore. It is made with strong black tea and has milk added to it. The tea tastes rich, as we use evaporated and condensed milk—lots of it too! I have suggested a tantalising spice mix here to make this cupcake thoroughly exotic!*

Teh Si Cupcakes makes 12 cupcakes

Tea bags (preferably strong black tea) 2

Boiling water 100 ml (3$\frac{1}{2}$ fl oz)

Full cream milk 4 Tbsp + more if desired

Evaporated milk 4 Tbsp

Unsalted butter 125 g (4$\frac{1}{2}$ oz)

Brown sugar 125 g (4$\frac{1}{2}$ oz)

Eggs 2, lightly beaten

Salt a pinch

Ground cinnamon (optional) $\frac{1}{2}$ tsp

Ground nutmeg (optional) $\frac{1}{2}$ tsp

Self-raising flour 150 g (5$\frac{1}{3}$ oz)

TOPPING

Whipped Topping cream (page 159) *or* **vanilla buttercream** (page 154) *or* **condensed milk glaze** (page 162)

Cinnamon sugar (optional) $\frac{1}{2}$ tsp ground cinnamon mixed with 2 tsp caster sugar

1. Place tea bags in boiling water in a small pot and let it simmer for 5 minutes. Add milk and evaporated milk and let it simmer over medium heat for another 5 minutes so that it reduces a bit. Remove from heat and set aside.
2. Preheat oven to 180°C (350°F). Line muffin tray with cupcake liners.
3. Cream butter in an electric mixer for a few minutes. Gradually add brown sugar and continue to beat until well combined.
4. Add eggs and beat until mixture is well blended, light and fluffy.
5. Add salt and, if using, cinnamon and nutmeg. Mix well.
6. Add flour and continue to beat until well mixed. Stop immediately once all the flour has been mixed well into the batter.
7. Discard tea bags and add milk tea to batter. Mix well.
8. Spoon batter into cupcake liners until three-quarters full. Bake for 20–25 minutes. Remove from oven and let cupcakes sit in muffin tray for 5 minutes.
9. Remove cupcakes from tray and place on a wire rack to cool completely before frosting.
10. Top cupcakes with desired frosting and garnish with cinnamon sugar if desired.

Note

- If you like chai or Masala tea, consider adding the following in place of $\frac{1}{2}$ tsp cinnamon and $\frac{1}{2}$ tsp nutmeg: A pinch of salt, a pinch of ground cardamom, $\frac{1}{2}$ tsp ground white pepper, $\frac{1}{2}$ tsp ground cinnamon, $\frac{1}{2}$ tsp ground ginger, 1 tsp ground clove (go easy on this one), 1 tsp nutmeg.

Milo Cupcakes makes 12 cupcakes

Self-raising flour 100 g (3½ oz)

Milo powder 4 Tbsp

Unsalted butter 125 g (4½ oz)

Brown sugar 125 g (4½ oz)

Eggs 2, lightly beaten

Evaporated milk 4 Tbsp

TOPPING

Whipped topping cream (page 159)

Milo powder

Mini marshmallows

1. Preheat oven to 180°C (350°F). Line muffin tray with cupcake liners. You may also bake the cupcakes in oven-safe mugs.
2. Sift flour and milo together in a bowl. Set aside.
3. Cream butter in an electric mixer for a few minutes. Gradually add brown sugar and continue to beat until well combined.
4. Add eggs and beat until mixture is well blended, light and fluffy.
5. Add flour and milo mixture prepared in step 2. Continue to beat until well mixed. Stop immediately once all the flour has been mixed well into the batter.
6. Add evaporated milk. Stir to mix well.
7. Spoon batter into cupcake liners or mugs until three-quarters full. Bake for 20–25 minutes. Remove from oven and let cupcakes sit in muffin tray for 5 minutes, then remove cupcakes from tray and place on a wire rack to cool completely before frosting. If using mugs, allow cupcakes to cool completely before frosting.
8. Gently spread a thick layer of whipped topping cream on top of cupcakes. Sift some milo powder over topping cream and garnish with mini marshmallows.

Note

- For a more intense Milo kick, increase the amount of Milo powder to 6 Tbsp!

Milo is a chocolate-malt beverage that is enjoyed around the world. Kids and adults will totally love this!

Horlicks Cupcakes makes 12–15 cupcakes

Horlicks powder 160 g
 (5^2/$_3$ oz)

Plain (all-purpose) flour 180 g
 (6^1/$_3$ oz)

Baking powder 2 tsp

Unsalted butter 300 g
 (10^1/$_2$ oz)

Caster sugar 100 g (3^1/$_2$ oz)

Eggs 4, lightly beaten

Sweetened condensed milk 200 ml (6^3/$_4$ fl oz)

Jam of choice to taste

1. Prepare a steamer or use a wok filled with enough boiling water.
2. Sift Horlicks powder, flour and baking powder together in a bowl. Set aside.
3. Cream butter in an electric mixer for a few minutes. Gradually add sugar and continue to beat until well combined.
4. Add eggs and beat until mixture is well blended, light and fluffy.
5. Add condensed milk and continue to beat until smooth.
6. Using a spatula, fold in Horlicks flour mixture prepared in step 2.
7. Spoon batter into waxed paper liners until two-thirds full. Place waxed liners on a plate. Cover with a sheet of aluminium foil and steam for 15–20 minutes.
8. Serve with a side of your favourite jam.

Note

- Covering the batter with aluminium foil before steaming prevents steam or condensation from coming into contact with the cupcakes. Be careful, however, to leave enough space between the aluminium foil and paper liners, or the batter will not rise properly and the cupcakes will collapse.
- If you like Horlicks, increase the amount to 180 g (6^1/$_3$ oz) for a stronger taste.

Kaya Surprise Cupcakes <small>makes 12 cupcakes</small>

Unsalted butter 125 g (4 1/2 oz)

Light brown sugar 150 g (5 1/3 oz)

Eggs 3, lightly beaten

Vanilla extract 1 tsp

Salt a pinch

Self-raising flour 150 g (5 1/3 oz)

Ground nutmeg 2 tsp

Heavy cream (optional) 3 Tbsp

KAYA MOUSSE

Topping cream 150 g (5 1/3 oz)

Coconut rum (optional) 1 Tbsp

Kaya 150 g (5 1/3 oz), at room temperature

1. Preheat oven to 180°C (350°F). Line muffin tray with cupcake liners.
2. Cream butter in an electric mixer for a few minutes. Gradually add brown sugar and continue to beat until well combined.
3. Add eggs and beat until mixture is well blended, light and fluffy.
4. Add vanilla extract and salt. Mix well.
5. Add flour and nutmeg. Continue to beat until well mixed. Stop immediately once all the flour has been mixed well into the batter.
6. Add heavy cream if using and mix well.
7. Spoon batter into cupcake liners until three-quarters full. Bake for 25 minutes or until cupcakes are golden brown and a toothpick inserted into the centre of cakes comes out clean. Remove from oven and let cupcakes sit in muffin tray for 10 minutes.
8. Remove cupcakes from tray and place on a wire rack to cool completely before frosting.
9. Prepare kaya mousse. In a chilled metal bowl, whisk topping cream at high speed until stiff peaks form. Stir in coconut rum if using.
10. Using a spatula, mix a small portion of cream with kaya. When well combined, add remaining cream and mix well. Add less cream if you prefer a thicker mousse.
11. Pipe kaya mousse over the cupcakes and serve.

This cupcake was inspired by my friend, Bryan, who loves kaya on toast. Kaya is a pandan-flavoured jam made from coconut cream and eggs. This sweet creamy spread is often eaten with bread or toast. In the olden days, kaya was laboriously cooked over slow fire. These days, it is available in supermarkets and speciality bakeries. In this recipe, the warm nutmeg cupcakes paired with rum-flavoured kaya mousse is an intoxicatingly Asian inspiration!

Spiced Mocha Madness makes 12 cupcakes

Plain (all-purpose) flour 125 g (4½ oz)

Baking powder 1 tsp

Baking soda 1 tsp

Semi-sweet chocolate couverture 75 g (2⅔ oz)

Unsalted butter 125 g (4½ oz), softened

Light brown sugar 125 g (4½ oz)

Eggs 2

Vanilla extract 1 tsp

Salt a pinch

Coffee granules 1 Tbsp, dissolved in 2 Tbsp hot water

Heavy cream 4 Tbsp

SPICE MIX

Ground ginger 1½ tsp

Ground cinnamon 1 tsp

Ground nutmeg a pinch

Ground clove a pinch

TOPPING

Dark chocolate ganache (page 146)

Chocolate crumble candy (optional)

1. Preheat oven to 180°C (350°F). Line muffin tray with cupcake liners.
2. Sift flour, baking powder, baking soda and spice mix together. Use a hand-held whisk to blend everything together.
3. Melt chocolate in a bowl placed over simmering water. Remove from heat when fully melted. Set aside.
4. Cream butter in an electric mixer for a few minutes. Gradually add brown sugar and continue to beat until well combined.
5. Add eggs and beat until mixture is well blended, light and fluffy.
6. Add vanilla extract, salt and coffee. Mix until well combined.
7. Add flour mixture prepared in step 2 and continue to beat. Combine with heavy cream. Stop immediately once all the flour and cream have been mixed well into the batter.
8. Using a spatula, fold in melted chocolate.
9. Spoon batter into cupcake liners until two-thirds full. Bake for 25 minutes or until a toothpick inserted into the centre of cakes comes out clean. Remove from oven and transfer cupcakes to a wire rack to cool completely before frosting.
10. Spread a generous layer of dark chocolate ganache on top of cupcakes. For an extra sweet treat, break some chocolate crumble candy over the ganache.

These spiced cupcakes are perfect for Christmas and any other time of the year! You will appreciate the spicy sensation in these cupcakes. Be generous with the nutmeg and clove.

Ginger Bro Cupcakes makes 15 cupcakes

Self-raising flour 150 g (5$\frac{1}{3}$ oz)

Salt a pinch

Ground ginger 1$\frac{1}{2}$ tsp

Ground nutmeg 1 tsp

Unsalted butter 125 g (4$\frac{1}{2}$ oz)

Dark brown sugar 125 g (4$\frac{1}{2}$ oz)

Eggs 2, lightly beaten

Vanilla extract 1 tsp

Sour cream or plain yoghurt 2 Tbsp

Grated ginger 1 tsp

Crystallised ginger 2 Tbsp, chopped

Walnuts 4 Tbsp, roughly chopped

TOPPING

Lemon-flavoured cream cheese frosting (page 149) *or* **lemon-flavoured royal icing** (page 158)

Store-bought gingernut cookies

Crystallised ginger

1. Preheat oven to 180°C (350°F). Line muffin tray with cupcake liners.
2. Combine flour, salt, ground ginger and nutmeg in a bowl and whisk to combine well.
3. Cream butter in an electric mixer for a few minutes. Gradually add dark brown sugar and continue to beat until well combined.
4. Add eggs and beat until mixture is well blended, light and fluffy.
5. Add vanilla extract, sour cream or yoghurt, and grated ginger. Mix well.
6. Add flour mixture prepared in step 2 and continue to beat until well mixed. Stop immediately once all the flour has been mixed well into the batter.
7. Using a spatula, fold in crystallised ginger and walnuts.
8. Spoon batter into cupcake liners until three-quarters full. Bake for 20–25 minutes. Remove from oven and let cupcakes sit in muffin tray for 5 minutes.
9. Remove cupcakes from tray and place on a wire rack to cool completely before frosting.
10. Frost cupcakes as desired. Top with store-bought ginger cookies and crystallised ginger.

I put a new spin on the traditional gingerbread cupcakes with the addition of walnuts and crystallised ginger. These can be enjoyed anytime of the year, not just during the festive season!

Yummy Orange Cardamom Cupcakes *makes 15 cupcakes*

Unsalted butter 125 g (4½ oz)

Light brown sugar 150 g (5⅓ oz)

Eggs 3, lightly beaten

Orange zest grated from 1 orange

Orange juice from 1 orange, pulp reserved if desired

Vanilla extract 1 tsp

Salt a pinch

Self-raising flour 150 g (5⅓ oz)

Ground cardamom 2 tsp *or* **cardamom essential oil** 5–7 drops

Full cream milk (optional) 2 Tbsp

TOPPING

Custard cream (page 157) *or* **orange glaze** (page 164) *or* **condensed milk glaze** (page 162)

1. Preheat oven to 180°C (350°F). Line muffin tray with cupcake liners.
2. Cream butter in an electric mixer for a few minutes. Gradually add brown sugar and continue to beat until well combined.
3. Add eggs and beat until mixture is well blended, light and fluffy.
4. Add orange zest, orange juice, vanilla extract and salt. Mix well.
5. Add flour and cardamom or cardamom essential oil. Continue to beat until well mixed. Stop immediately once all the flour has been mixed well into the batter.
6. Add milk if using and mix well.
7. Spoon batter into cupcake liners until three-quarters full. Bake for 20–25 minutes. Remove from oven and let cupcakes sit in muffin tray for 5 minutes.
8. Remove cupcakes from tray and place on a wire rack to cool completely before frosting.
9. Garnish with a dollop of custard cream. Alternatively, spoon orange glaze or condensed milk glaze over the cupcakes.

Note

- If using ground cardamom, grind it fresh from pods for the best flavour. Split open 10 pods and discard the husks. Grind the seeds with a pestle and mortar. This should yield 2 tsp ground cardamom.

Cardamom is an exotic spice often used in India, Bhutan and the Nordic countries. Green cardamom (as opposed to black or brown) tends to be prized among those in the know, and its sweet resinous aroma is suitable for making desserts. But in the interest of convenience and efficiency, cardamom essential oil is best, while ground cardamom is a good alternative to pounding fresh cardamom. The imaginative combination of orange and cardamom makes these cupcakes thoroughly enjoyable for afternoon tea or post-dinner dessert!

Lemongrass is naturally sweet, uplifting and lightly citrusy. It is typically used in Asian cooking for curries, teas and soups. I have paired these lemongrass cupcakes with coconut cream to make them gorgeously delicious. I like to use lemongrass essential oil as it is so convenient, and the aroma and taste are so intense despite adding only a few drops!

Lemongrass Cupcakes makes 12 cupcakes

Coconut milk 100 ml (3$^1/_3$ fl oz)

Lemongrass essential oil or essence 5–10 drops

Unsalted butter 125 g (4$^1/_2$ oz)

Caster sugar 125 g (4$^1/_2$ oz)

Eggs 2, lightly beaten

Self-raising flour 150 g (5$^1/_3$ oz)

Vanilla extract $^1/_2$ tsp

Salt a pinch

TOPPING

Vanilla buttercream (page 154)

Desiccated coconut

Store-bought nata de coco

1. Prepare lemongrass-infused coconut milk. Combine coconut milk and lemongrass essential oil or essence. Stir well and set aside.
2. Preheat oven to 180°C (350°F). Line muffin tray with cupcake liners.
3. Cream butter in an electric mixer for a few minutes. Gradually add sugar and continue to beat until well combined.
4. Add eggs and beat until mixture is well blended, light and fluffy.
5. Add flour and continue to beat until well mixed. Stop immediately once all the flour has been mixed well into the batter.
6. Add lemongrass-infused coconut milk, vanilla extract and salt. Mix well.
7. Spoon batter into cupcake liners until three-quarters full. Bake for 20–25 minutes. Remove from oven and let cupcakes sit in muffin tray for 5 minutes.
8. Remove cupcakes from tray and place on a wire rack to cool completely before frosting.
9. Top cupcakes with vanilla buttercream and sprinkle with a generous amount of desiccated coconut. Garnish with cubes of store-bought nata de coco.

Note

- This is an alternative way to prepare lemongrass-infused coconut milk: Add 1 stalk of lemongrass into 125 ml (4 fl oz / $^1/_2$ cup) coconut milk in a saucepan. Bring to a slow boil and let it simmer for 3–5 minutes over low heat. Transfer to a blender and pulse for 30 seconds. Strain and let it cool before use.

alcoholic concoctions that jazz up any occasion

brandy raisin cupcakes	116
pina colada cupcakes	118
yo dudes	120
almond dream cupcakes	123
gold rush cupcakes	124
oranginal sin	126
ye ye stout cupcakes	128
choya chill	130
pimm's no. 1 cup	132
james bond cupcakes	135
mojito calling	136
screwdriver cupcakes	138
pear and port cupcakes	140
hot and dirty go pop	142

Brandy Raisin Cupcakes makes 12 cupcakes

Dried raisins 75 g (2$^{2}/_{3}$ oz)

Brandy 4 Tbsp

Unsalted butter 125 g (4$^{1}/_{2}$ oz)

Caster sugar 125 g (4$^{1}/_{2}$ oz)

Eggs 2, lightly beaten

Self-raising flour 150 g (5$^{1}/_{3}$ oz) + 1 Tbsp for sifting over raisins

BRANDY SYRUP

Brandy 5 Tbsp

Light brown sugar 2 tsp

TOPPING

Rose-scented no-bake meringue (page 167)

1. Soak raisins in brandy overnight or for at least 2–3 hours.
2. Preheat oven to 180°C (350°F). Line muffin tray with cupcake liners.
3. Cream butter in an electric mixer for a few minutes. Gradually add sugar and continue to beat until well combined.
4. Add eggs and beat until mixture is well blended, light and fluffy.
5. Add flour and continue to beat until well mixed. Stop immediately once all the flour has been mixed well into the batter.
6. Sift 1 Tbsp self-raising flour over brandied raisins. Using a spatula, fold brandy-soaked raisins into the batter.
7. Spoon batter into cupcake liners until three-quarters full. Bake for 20 minutes. Remove from oven.
8. While cupcakes are baking, prepare brandy syrup. Simmer brandy and sugar in a saucepan for about 5 minutes until mixture thickens and is reduced slightly.
9. Upon removal of the cupcakes from the oven, use a toothpick to pierce several holes in cupcakes. Using a teaspoon, drizzle brandy syrup over cupcakes.
10. Remove cupcakes from tray and place on a wire rack to cool completely before frosting.
11. Pipe rose-scented no-bake meringue over cupcakes.

Note

- For a more intense alcoholic flavour, instead of brandy syrup, omit the sugar and heating, and just use brandy. This is more lethal, and I certainly approve of it!

These cupcakes are easy to make, yet they are totally desirable. Guests and future in-laws will be suitably impressed with them, especially when you top the cupcakes with the fragrant rose-scented no-bake meringue. Be warned, people will be clamouring for these babies!

Pina Colada Cupcakes <small>makes 12 cupcakes</small>

Unsalted butter 100 g (3½ oz)

Caster sugar 125 g (4½ oz)

Eggs 2, lightly beaten

Coconut cream 125 ml (4 fl oz / ½ cup)

Coconut-flavoured rum 2 Tbsp + more to drizzle over baked cupcakes

Self-raising flour 150 g (5⅓ oz) + 1 Tbsp for sifting over pineapples

Cornflour (cornstarch) 1 tsp

Canned pineapples 100 g (3½ oz), drained and cubed

TOPPING

Coconut-rum frosting (page 166)

1. Preheat oven to 190°C (375°F). Line muffin tray with cupcake liners.
2. Cream butter in an electric mixer for a few minutes. Gradually add sugar and continue to beat until well combined.
3. Add eggs and beat until mixture is well blended, light and fluffy.
4. Add coconut cream and rum. Mix well.
5. Add flour and cornflour. Continue to beat until well mixed. Stop immediately once all the flour has been mixed well into the batter.
6. Sift 1 Tbsp self-raising flour over pineapples. Using a spatula, fold pineapples into the batter.
7. Spoon batter into cupcake liners until three-quarters full. Bake for 20 minutes. (Watch the oven to ensure that cupcakes are not over baked. The cupcakes should appear light yellow and dry.)
8. Remove cupcakes from the oven and place a wire rack to cool completely before frosting.
9. Using a toothpick, pierce several holes in the cupcakes and drizzle over with some coconut-flavoured rum.
10. Top with coconut-rum frosting. Use the back of a spoon to spread frosting evenly over cupcakes.

These are perfect sweets on a hot afternoon, especially after a dip in the pool. Or if you are missing the tropics or the beach, these are the cupcakes you will want to make. They are fun, frivolous, great for parties and yummy!

Yo Dudes makes 12 cupcakes

Unsalted butter 125 g (4½ oz)

Caster sugar 125 g (4½ oz)

Eggs 2, lightly beaten

Vanilla extract 1 tsp

Salt a pinch

Self-raising flour 150 g (5⅓ oz)

Beer 125 ml (4 fl oz / ½ cup)

TOPPING

Salted cream cheese frosting (page 149)

Mini pretzels

1. Preheat oven to 180°C (350°F). Line muffin tray with cupcake liners.
2. Cream butter in an electric mixer for a few minutes. Gradually add sugar and continue to beat until well combined.
3. Add eggs and beat until mixture is well blended, light and fluffy.
4. Add vanilla extract and salt. Mix well.
5. Add flour and continue to beat until well mixed. Stop immediately once all the flour has been mixed well into the batter.
6. Spoon batter into cupcake liners until three-quarters full. Bake for 20–25 minutes. Remove from oven and let cupcakes sit in muffin tray for 5 minutes.
7. Remove cupcakes from tray and place on a wire rack to cool.
8. Using a toothpick, pierce several holes in the cupcakes while they are still warm. Drizzle beer over cupcakes. Cool completely before frosting.
9. Pipe swirls of salted cream cheese frosting on top of cupcakes. Top with mini pretzels. And don't forget the cold beer in an iced mug!

Note
- If you are generous with the beer, consider using foil-laminated liners as these will hold the beer better.

Best consumed during a football game or when testosterones are called for! Can't get enough of the beer taste? Choose darker coloured beers and lagers that have a stronger flavour and a higher alcohol content, although they may also be a bit more bitter. Drench (I mean drizzle!) the baked cupcakes with beer! Don't drink and drive though.

I particularly like the comforting and slightly sweet taste of almond. And Amaretto, being almond-flavoured liqueur, makes it extra special! So baking these Almond Dream cupcakes was a natural choice for me.

Almond Dream Cupcakes <small>makes 12 cupcakes</small>

Unsalted butter 125 g (4½ oz)

Caster sugar 125 g (4½ oz)

Eggs 2, lightly beaten

Vanilla extract ½ tsp

Almond essence 1 tsp

Self-raising flour 125 g (4½ oz)

Amaretto 2 Tbsp + more for drizzling over cupcakes

TOPPING

Whipped topping cream (page 159)

Toasted almond flakes *or* cornflakes

1. Preheat oven to 180°C (350°F). Line muffin tray with foil-laminated cupcake liners.
2. Cream butter in an electric mixer for a few minutes. Gradually add sugar and continue to beat until well combined.
3. Add eggs and beat until mixture is well blended, light and fluffy.
4. Add vanilla extract and almond essence. Mix well.
5. Add flour and continue to beat until well mixed. Stop immediately once all the flour has been mixed well into the batter.
6. Add Amaretto and mix well.
7. Spoon batter into cupcake liners until three-quarters full. Bake for 20–25 minutes. Remove from oven and let cupcakes sit in muffin tray for 5 minutes.
8. Remove cupcakes from tray and place on a wire rack to cool.
9. Using a toothpick, pierce several holes in the cupcakes while they are still warm. Drizzle Amaretto over the cupcakes. Cool completely before frosting.
10. Spoon whipped topping cream over the cupcakes. Garnish with toasted almond flakes. Alternatively, use cornflakes if you do not have almond flakes in your kitchen.

Note

- If you are generous with Amaretto, consider using foil-laminated liners as these will hold the liqueur better.
- For almond fans, there are two things you can do to up the ante on these cupcakes. Firstly, consider adding 3 Tbsp almond meal into the self-raising flour. This way, you can get up to 15 cupcakes, depending on the size of the cupcake liners, as well as a denser texture. Secondly, fold 50 g (1⅔ oz) almond flakes into the batter if desired. This adds crunchiness and extra nuttiness.

Gold Rush Cupcakes makes 12 cupcakes

Unsalted butter 125 g (4½ oz)

Caster sugar 125 g (4½ oz)

Eggs 2, lightly beaten

Orange oil 1 tsp *or* **orange essential oil** 5 drops

Orange juice from ½ orange

Orange zest grated from ½ orange

Self-raising flour 125 g (4½ oz)

Orange liqueur (Grand Marnier) 2 Tbsp + more for drizzling

TOPPING

Vanilla-orange liqueur buttercream (page 154) *or* **orange glaze** (page 164)

Edible gold paper (optional)

1. Preheat oven to 180°C (350°F). Line muffin tray with cupcake liners.
2. Cream butter in an electric mixer for a few minutes. Gradually add sugar and continue to beat until well combined.
3. Add eggs and beat until mixture is well blended, light and fluffy.
4. Add orange oil or essential oil, juice and zest. Mix well.
5. Add flour and continue to beat until well mixed. Stop immediately once all the flour has been mixed well into the batter.
6. Add orange liqueur and mix well.
7. Spoon batter into cupcake liners until three-quarters full. Bake for 20–25 minutes. Remove from oven and let cupcakes sit in muffin tray for 5 minutes.
8. Remove cupcakes from tray and place on a wire rack to cool.
9. Using a toothpick, pierce several holes in the cupcakes while they are still warm. Drizzle orange liqueur over the cupcakes. Cool completely before frosting.
10. Pipe a dollop of vanilla-orange liqueur buttercream on top of cupcakes. Garnish buttercream with a flake of edible gold paper if desired. Alternatively, spoon orange glaze over and garnish with flakes of edible gold paper.

To many Asians, orange symbolises abundance, gold and wealth, making these cupcakes particularly appropriate for festive occasions. The gold flakes add a touch of opulence to the cupcakes.

Oranginal Sin makes 12 cupcakes

Self-raising flour 125 g (4½ oz)

Cocoa powder 2 Tbsp

Unsalted butter 125 g (4½ oz)

Dark brown sugar 125 g (4½ oz)

Eggs 2

Vanilla extract 1 tsp

Orange oil 1 tsp *or* **orange essential oil** 5 drops

Orange liqueur (Grand Marnier) 2 Tbsp

Orange zest grated from 1 orange

TOPPING

Orange liqueur-flavoured chocolate ganache (page 146)

Orange zest

1. Preheat oven to 180°C (350°F). Line muffin tray with cupcake liners.
2. Sift flour and cocoa powder together. Set aside.
3. Cream butter in an electric mixer for a few minutes. Gradually add dark brown sugar and continue to beat until well combined.
4. Add eggs and beat until mixture is well blended, light and fluffy.
5. Add vanilla extract, orange oil or essential oil, liqueur and zest. Mix well.
6. Add flour and cocoa mixture prepared in step 2. Continue to beat until well mixed. Stop immediately once all the flour has been mixed well into the batter.
7. Spoon batter into cupcake liners until three-quarters full. Bake for 20–25 minutes. Remove from oven and let cupcakes sit in muffin tray for 5 minutes.
8. Remove cupcakes from tray and place on a wire rack to cool completely before frosting.
9. Spread a thick layer of orange liqueur-flavoured chocolate ganache on top of cupcakes. Sprinkle orange zest randomly over the ganache before serving.

Note
- For a more chocolaty taste, add up to 3 Tbsp cocoa powder, or add 2 Tbsp mini chocolate chips. Fold in the chips after step 6 with the help of a spatula.

A wonderful combination of sweet orange and seductive dark chocolate makes for a nice ending to a romantic dinner. Orange liqueur adds to the decadence and makes the cupcakes more irresistible!

Ye Ye Stout Cupcakes makes 12 cupcakes

Cocoa powder 4 Tbsp

Plain (all-purpose) flour 160 g (5^2/$_3$ oz)

Baking soda ½ tsp

Salt a pinch

Caster sugar 225 g (8 oz)

Unsalted butter 65 g (2^1/$_3$ oz), softened

Stout ½ can or 165 ml (5^2/$_3$ fl oz) (Save the remaining stout to make the glaze)

Vanilla extract 1 tsp

Eggs 2, lightly beaten

Sour cream *or* **heavy cream** 4 Tbsp

TOPPING

Stout glaze (page 162) *or* **stout buttercream** (page 154) *or* **whisky buttercream** (page 154)

1. Preheat oven to 180°C (350°F). Line muffin tray with cupcake liners.
2. Sift cocoa powder, flour, baking soda and salt together. Combine mixture with sugar in a bowl and mix well using a hand-held whisk. Set aside.
3. Cream butter in a separate bowl. Add stout and vanilla extract. Mix well.
4. Add eggs and sour cream or yoghurt. Continue to beat until well combined and smooth.
5. Add flour mixture prepared in step 2 and continue to beat until all the ingredients are well blended.
6. Spoon batter into cupcake liners until three-quarters full. Bake for 20–25 minutes. Remove from oven and let cupcakes sit in muffin tray for 5 minutes.
7. Remove cupcakes and place on a wire rack to cool. Cool completely before frosting.
8. Dunk cupcakes in stout glaze before serving. Alternatively, top with stout buttercream or, for something really decadent, whisky buttercream.

My late grandfather (Ye Ye) was a carpenter and he loved having stout over his meals. He also had a sweet tooth. Whenever I make these cupcakes, I think of how much I miss him. I'm sure he would love these cupcakes if he were still around.

Choya Chill makes 12 servings

MASCARPONE CHEESE FILLING

Eggs 2, yolks and whites separated

Caster sugar 80 g (2⁴/₅ oz)

Mascarpone cheese 250 g (9 oz)

Heavy cream 100 g (3½ oz)

ASSEMBLY

Green tea powder 3 tsp + more for garnishing

Hot water 100 ml (3⅓ fl oz)

Choya 4–6 Tbsp

Store-bought finger sponge biscuits 12, each broken into 2–3 pieces

MASCARPONE CHEESE FILLING

1. In a bowl, beat egg yolks and half the sugar until pale and fluffy. Add mascarpone cheese and ensure that all is well combined. (You may use a paddle attachment to do this if using a cake mixer.)
2. Using an electric mixer fitted with a whisk attachment, whip heavy cream in a chilled metal bowl until stiff peaks form. You can also place the chilled metal bowl over a bigger bowl filled with ice cubes.
3. Using a spatula, fold whipped heavy cream into mascarpone mixture prepared in step 1.
4. Beat egg whites and remaining sugar in an electric mixer on high speed until glossy and soft peaks form. Fold into mixture prepared in step 3.

ASSEMBLY

5. Prepare Choya-green tea. Dissolve 3 tsp green tea powder in hot water. Combine with Choya and stir to mix well.
6. Spoon 1 Tbsp mascarpone cheese filling into a cup or ramekin.
7. Dip a piece of finger sponge biscuit into Choya-green tea and arrange on top of mascarpone cheese filling.
8. Top with another layer of mascarpone cheese filling and dust green tea powder over.
9. Repeat steps 7–8 until cup or ramekin is full.
10. Chill in the refrigerator for at least 30 minutes before serving.

Note

- When whisking egg whites, I recommend using a cake mixer with a whisk attachment.

Choya is a Japanese plum liqueur that I simply adore, and very often I will have it while sitting by my balcony overlooking the city. It relaxes me and puts me in a good mood.

I have incorporated Choya with green tea to give you this sensational dessert. Be sure to make extra for your guests and loved ones, as one is never enough! This is a no-bake alcoholic dessert, which is simple to assemble, and best eaten with a spoon.

Pimm's No. 1 Cup makes 12 cupcakes

Butter 125 g (4$^1/_2$ oz)

Light brown sugar 125 g (4$^1/_2$ oz)

Eggs 2, lightly beaten

Orange oil 1 tsp *or* **orange essential oil** 5 drops

Pimm's liqueur 3 Tbsp + more for garnishing

Self-raising flour 125 g (4$^1/_2$ oz)

PIMM'S JELLY

Strawberries 3, hulled and roughly chopped

Orange 1 segment, roughly chopped

Cucumber 2-cm (1-in) length, roughly chopped

Peppermint leaf 1, large, roughly chopped

Pimm's liqueur 100 ml (3$^1/_3$ fl oz)

Ice cubes 100 ml (3$^1/_3$ fl oz)

Gelatine powder 6 tsp *or* **gelatine sheets** 2 *or* **agar agar powder** 5 g ($^1/_6$ oz)

Lemon-lime soda 250 ml (8 fl oz / 1 cup)

TOPPING

Lemon-mint buttercream (page 154)

Pimm's jelly

Strawberry slices

Slivers of cucumber

1. Prepare Pimm's jelly a day in advance. Preheat oven to 180°C (350°F). Line muffin tray with cupcake liners.
2. Cream butter in an electric mixer for a few minutes. Gradually add sugar and continue to beat until all the sugar has blended into the butter.
3. Add eggs and beat until everything is well blended, such that it is now light and fluffy.
4. Mix in orange oil or essential oil and liqueur.
5. Add flour and continue to beat until well mixed. Stop immediately once all the flour has been mixed well into the batter.
6. Spoon batter into cupcake liners until three-quarters full. Bake for 20–25 minutes. Remove from oven and let cupcakes sit in muffin tray for 5 minutes.
7. Remove cupcakes from tray and place on a wire rack to cool completely before frosting.
8. Using a toothpick, pierce several holes in the cupcakes while they are still warm. Drizzle some liqueur over the cupcakes. Cool completely before frosting.
9. Spread a layer of lemon-mint buttercream over the cupcakes. Top with Pimm's jelly, strawberry slices and slivers of cucumber. Serve with a tall glass of Pimm's cocktail!

PIMM'S JELLY (Prepare a day in advance.)

1. Prepare Pimm's cocktail. Put strawberries, orange, cucumber and peppermint leaf in a cocktail mixer. Add Pimm's and ice cubes, and shake vigorously. Drain into a glass, removing all the pulp. Set aside.
2. Prepare jelly base. Follow packet instructions of gelatine or agar agar powder. Use lemon-lime soda instead of water as liquid for boiling. Remove from heat when fully dissolved. Add to Pimm's cocktail and stir well.
3. Pour into plastic moulds of your choice and refrigerate. Once set, remove jelly from mould and cut into rectangular cubes. The jelly should be firm and easy to handle. Set aside.

Inspired by one of my favourite cocktail drinks, these cupcakes are perfect for any occasion, or if you simply want to indulge. Topping it off with Pimm's-flavoured jelly adds drama and attracts curiosity!

Dedicated to the man who popularised the "shaken, not stirred" Martini, these cupcakes bring debonair and style to new heights! You can use (more) vodka or gin in these cupcakes if you wish, but Martini Bianco is a must!

James Bond Cupcakes *makes 12 cupcakes*

Unsalted butter 125 g (4½ oz)

Caster sugar 125 g (4½ oz)

Eggs 2, lightly beaten

Vanilla extract 1 tsp

Salt a pinch

Self-raising flour 125 g (4½ oz)

Vodka 5 Tbsp

Martini Bianco 2 Tbsp

MARTINI-SPIKED LEMON-FLAVOURED TOPPING

Vodka 5 Tbsp

Martini Bianco 2 Tbsp

Lemon zest long, thin strips grated from 1 lemon

Lemon oil ½ tsp *or* **lemon essential oil** 3 drops

Whipped topping cream 1 portion (page 159)

1. Preheat oven to 180°C (350°F). Line muffin tray with cupcake liners.
2. Cream butter in an electric mixer for a few minutes. Gradually add sugar and continue to beat until well combined.
3. Add eggs and beat until mixture is well blended, light and fluffy.
4. Add vanilla extract and salt. Mix well.
5. Add flour and continue to beat until well mixed. Stop immediately once all the flour has been mixed well into the batter.
6. Spoon batter into cupcake liners until three-quarters full. Bake for 20–25 minutes. Remove from oven and let cupcakes sit in muffin tray for 5 minutes.
7. Mix vodka and Martini Bianco in a cup. Using a toothpick, pierce several holes in cupcakes and drizzle mixed alcohol over. Cool completely before frosting.
8. Spoon a dollop of martini-spiked lemon-flavoured whipped cream on top and garnish with marinated lemon zest.

MARTINI-SPIKED LEMON-FLAVOURED TOPPING

1. Prepare marinated lemon zest a day ahead. Mix vodka and Martini Bianco. Soak lemon zest in it overnight.
2. Drain zest. Use zest for garnishing and reserve drained alochol.
3. Blend drained alcohol and lemon oil or essential oil into whipped topping cream.

Note

- If you are adventurous, consider mixing 5 Tbsp vodka, 1 Tbsp brandy and 1 Tbsp peach juice (or pineapple juice) for drizzling over the cupcakes. Reserve some of this cocktail to flavour the whipped topping cream.

Mojito Calling makes 12 servings

Salted pretzels 100–120 g
   (3$\frac{1}{2}$ oz–4$\frac{1}{3}$ oz)

Unsalted butter 200 g (7 oz)

Caster sugar 3 Tbsp

Cream cheese 500 g
   (1 lb 1$\frac{1}{2}$ oz)

Icing (confectioner's) sugar
   100 g (3$\frac{1}{2}$ oz)

Lime zest grated from 3 limes

Lime juice 5 Tbsp

White rum 3 Tbsp

Heavy cream 350 g (12$\frac{1}{2}$ oz)

TOPPING

Mint leaves

1. Process pretzels in a blender into powder. Alternatively, place the pretzels in a resealable plastic bag and crush them into powder using a rolling pin.

2. Melt butter in a saucepan. Stir in crushed pretzels and sugar. Cook over medium heat and stir until sugar has dissolved. Remove from heat and leave to cool for 15 minutes.

3. When cooled, press 2 Tbsp pretzel mixture into the bottom of each cup in a muffin tray to form a pretzel base. Freeze for at least 30 minutes.

4. In the meantime, prepare cream cheese mixture. Using an electric mixer with a paddle attachment, beat cream cheese on medium speed for about 3 minutes. Add half the icing sugar and continue to beat until well combined. Add remaining icing sugar and continue to beat, ensuring that icing sugar is well incorporated. The resultant mixture should be soft.

5. Combine with lime zest, lime juice and rum.

6. In a chilled metal bowl, beat heavy cream with a hand-held electric mixer until stiff peaks form. Fold into cream cheese mixture.

7. Top each pretzel base with cream cheese mixture. Tap tray and smooth the tops to prevent loosely packed portions. Cover with cling wrap and freeze for at least 6 hours, preferably overnight.

8. To serve, dip a small knife in hot water and run it around each cupcake. Invert cupcakes onto a clean surface. Garnish with mint leaves and serve immediately.

Note

- Lining the muffin tray with cupcake liners will make it easier to remove these desserts.
- If desired, spoon the cream cheese mixture into a piping bag for piping it over the pretzel base. This will ensure that the process is neat and tidy.
- The cupcakes are more savoury than sweet. If you prefer a sweeter concoction, increase the amount of icing sugar to 130 g (4$\frac{2}{3}$ oz) when preparing cream cheese mixture.

This is cocktail in a cake, for my friend, Edmund, who always orders a Mojito whenever he hits the bars! You can use pretzels or any salted biscuit for the base. The best thing about this recipe is that no baking is required!

Screwdriver Cupcakes makes 12 cupcakes

Unsalted butter 125 g (4½ oz)

Caster sugar 125 g (4½ oz)

Eggs 2, lightly beaten

Orange juice from ½ orange

Orange zest grated from ½ orange

Orange oil 1 tsp

Self-raising flour 125 g (4½ oz)

Vodka 5 Tbsp

TOPPING

Orange-vodka glaze (page 164)

Orange slices

1. Preheat oven to 180°C (350°F). Line muffin tray with cupcake liners.
2. Cream butter in an electric mixer for a few minutes. Gradually add sugar and continue to beat until well combined.
3. Add eggs and beat until mixture is well blended, light and fluffy.
4. Add orange juice, zest and orange oil. Mix well.
5. Add flour and continue to beat until well mixed. Stop immediately once all the flour has been mixed well into the batter.
6. Spoon batter into cupcake liners until three-quarters full. Bake for 20–25 minutes. Remove from oven and let cupcakes sit in muffin tray for 5 minutes.
7. Using a toothpick, pierce several holes in cupcakes and drizzle vodka over.
8. Remove cupcakes from tray and place on a wire rack to cool completely before frosting.
9. Drizzle orange-vodka glaze over cupcakes and top with orange slices.

VARIATIONS

- Caribbean screwdriver cupcakes: Mix 3 Tbsp vodka and 2 Tbsp Malibu (or coconut rum) for cupcake drizzle. Top with orange buttercream (page 154). Sprinkle over desiccated coconut before serving.

- California screwdriver cupcakes: Mix 3 Tbsp vodka and 2 Tbsp orange liqueur (Grand Marnier) for cupcake drizzle. Top with either orange-vodka glaze (page 164) or orange buttercream (page 154). Garnish with orange slices and red cherries.

- Power screwdriver cupcakes: Mix 3 Tbsp vodka and 3 Tbsp Coca-Cola for cupcake drizzle. Top with orange or Coca-Cola buttercream (page 154).

- Tequila screwdriver cupcakes: Replace vodka with tequila for cupcake drizzle. Top with tequila-spiked orange glaze (page 164).

Eat a cocktail; the perennial alcoholic drink is presented here as cupcakes, ideal for a lazy afternoon, party or chichi event. These cupcakes are simply baked with orange juice and liqueur. Get creative when you serve these cupcakes to impress your guests. Garnish as desired and maybe serve the cupcakes in tumblers!

Pear and Port Cupcakes makes 12 cupcakes

Unsalted butter 125 g (4½ oz)

Light brown sugar 125 g (4½ oz)

Eggs 2, lightly beaten

Vanilla extract 1 tsp

Ground cinnamon 1 tsp

Self-raising flour 125 g (4½ oz) + 1 Tbsp more for sifting over pears

Heavy cream 2 Tbsp

Port syrup 2 Tbsp

TOPPING

Port-infused cream cheese (page 149)

Poached pear slices

POACHED PEARS

Green Anjou pears 2, peeled and stalks removed

Port 250 ml (8 fl oz / 1 cup)

Water 4 Tbsp

Light brown sugar 30 g (1 oz)

Cinnamon 1 stick *or* **ground cinnamon** ¼ tsp

Lemon essential oil 6 drops *or* **lemon oil** ½ tsp

Salt a pinch

1. Prepare poached pears at least a day ahead. Preheat oven to 180°C (350°F). Line muffin tray with cupcake liners.
2. Cream butter in an electric mixer for a few minutes. Gradually add brown sugar and continue to beat until well combined.
3. Add eggs and beat until mixture is well blended, light and fluffy.
4. Mix in vanilla extract and ground cinnamon.
5. Add flour and continue to beat until well mixed. Stop immediately once well combined.
6. Mix in heavy cream and port syrup until well combined. Sift 1 Tbsp self-raising flour over pears. Using a spatula, fold cubed pears into the batter.
7. Spoon batter into cupcake liners until three-quarters full. Bake for 20–25 minutes. Remove from oven and let cupcakes sit in muffin tray for 5 minutes.
8. Remove cupcakes from tray and place on a wire rack to cool completely before frosting.
9. Pipe a generous amount of port-infused cream cheese on top of cupcakes. Using a toothpick, secure reserved wedges of poached pears over the frosting.

POACHED PEARS (Prepare at least a day in advance.)

1. Slice off pear bottoms so that they can stand. Half the pears and remove cores with a melon scoop. Cut each pear into 8 wedges.
2. Add all ingredients except pears in a saucepan. Bring to a boil over high heat, ensuring sugar and ground cinnamon (if using in place of cinnamon stick) are completely dissolved.
3. Add pears to the boiling mixture. Reduce heat to a simmer. Turn pears occasionally. Cook for 30 minutes. If you like the pears softer, cook for a longer time.
4. Allow pears to cool in poaching liquid (port syrup). Once cooled, remove cinnamon stick (if using). Keep in an airtight container and refrigerate overnight. The port syrup can be kept for up to 1 week.
5. Cut 4 wedges of poached pear into cubes for adding to cupcakes. Leave others whole for topping.

My good friend, Ernest, who has tasted cupcakes across the world and possesses an unyieldingly scrupulous standard in law (and taste, he professes), insisted I make him pear and port cupcakes. Dedicated to Ernest, these cupcakes are laborious to make but they are well worth the effort; they are a sight to behold and divine to the taste buds! For a non-alcoholic version of this cupcake, substitute raspberry (or mixed berry) tea for the port. By the way, Ernest convulsed in pleasure when he tasted these cupcakes.

Hot and Dirty Go Pop makes about 50 cake pops

Unsalted butter 125 g (4½ oz)

Caster sugar 125 g (4½ oz)

Eggs 2, lightly beaten

Orange juice from ½ orange

Orange zest grated from ½ orange

Orange oil 1 tsp

Black peppercorns 1 Tbsp, finely ground

Self-raising flour 125 g (4½ oz), sifted

Vanilla buttercream (page 154) 200 g (7 oz)

Vodka 4 Tbsp

VODKA-INFUSED WHIPPED CREAM

Heavy cream 500 g (1 lb 1½ oz)

Icing (confectioner's) sugar 6 Tbsp, sifted

Vodka 4 Tbsp + more if desired

Orange food colouring (optional) a few drops

Note

- Add more icing sugar to the whipped cream if desired.
- If the whipped cream is too soft or wet, add more icing sugar and continue beating at high speed. If too stiff, add more vodka.

1. Preheat oven to 180°C (350°F). Line a 20-cm (8-in) round cake tin with parchment paper.
2. Cream butter in an electric mixer for a few minutes. Gradually add sugar and continue to beat until well combined.
3. Add eggs and beat until mixture is well blended, light and fluffy.
4. Add orange juice, zest, orange oil and peppercorns. Mix well.
5. Add flour and continue to beat until well mixed. Stop immediately once well combined.
6. Pour batter into cake tin and bake for 35 minutes or more. Test doneness with a toothpick inserted into the centre of the cake—the toothpick should come out clean.
7. Remove from the oven and leave cake in tin for 10 minutes. Remove cake from tin and place on a wire rack to cool completely.
8. Once cooled, cut cake into big pieces and crumble into a big bowl.
9. Add half of the vanilla buttercream and vodka into crumbled cake. Use a cake mixer to blend or you can use your hands. Add remaining buttercream and continue blending. Ensure that mixture is not too wet or mushy. The resultant cake mixture should be crumbly.
10. Roll cake mixture into balls, each no bigger than 2.5 cm (1-in) in diameter, and place them on a baking sheet lined with parchment paper. Chill for at least 2 hours.
11. Prepare vodka-infused whipped cream. Using a whisk attachment, beat heavy cream on high speed, slowly adding icing sugar along the way. Add vodka once the cream gains volume and forms stiff peaks. Add more vodka if desired. However, do note that too much liquid will result in a wet and less voluminous texture.
12. Divide vodka-infused whipped cream into two portions. Add orange food colouring to one portion.
13. Drop a cake ball at the bottom of a champagne glass. Pipe vodka-infused whipped cream over cake ball, alternating between the non-coloured and coloured cream. Drop another 2–3 cake balls and cover with vodka-infused whipped cream. Alternate layers of vodka-infused whipped cream and cake balls until glass is three-quarters full. Serve immediately.

This recipe came about when my friend Nick brought me to a local Martini bar that supposedly serves the best martinis in town. I was inspired by the martinis and decided to create these peppery orange cake balls saturated with vodka (or your choice of poison, as some would say). Serve them on a stick to make cake pops, but I prefer to serve them in classy champagne flutes. Perfect ending to a date!

At the Top

frostings that bring your cupcakes to the next level

dark chocolate ganache	146	whipped heavy cream	160
white chocolate gananche	148	condensed milk glaze	162
cream cheese frosting	149	stout glaze	162
mascarpone frostings	150	kiwi glaze	163
buttercream frosting	152	orange glaze	164
strawberry buttercream	155	orange vodka glaze	164
chocolate buttercream	156	tofu frosting	165
custard cream	157	coconut rum frosting	166
royal icing	158	sea salt caramel frosting	166
whipped topping cream	159	no-bake meringue	167

Dark Chocolate Ganache for 12–15 cupcakes

For me, this is the pièce de résistance among all the frostings here. It tastes glorious with any baked treat or cake, and I can even eat it on its own! If there is any extra left, I eat it with bread, ice cream and whatever I fancy. I often serve this ganache with cupcakes, and my guests never fail to lap it all up! The consistency of the prepared ganache at room temperature is like thick spreadable jam, and it is perfect for layering on top of cupcakes.

It keeps its shape well and is suitable for piping intricate designs too. The recipe here is flexible. If you like a pouring consistency, add more cream or honey. Alternatively, pop the ganache into the microwave oven or leave it in the warm kitchen for it to get soft. Use the best chocolate available, and this will ensure an orgasmic culinary experience!

Heavy cream 140 g (5 fl oz)

Semi-sweet chocolate 200 g (7 oz), chopped

Honey (optional) 2 Tbsp

Glucose (optional) 2 Tbsp

Orange liqueur (optional) 2 Tbsp

Orange oil (optional) 2 tsp or 1 Tbsp for a stronger flavour

1. Heat heavy cream in a saucepan and bring to a gentle boil. Remove from heat immediately to prevent over-boiling or burning the cream.
2. Add chocolate and stir well with a hand-held whisk until all the chocolate has melted.
3. Add honey if using and continue to stir. The honey adds shine to the ganache.
4. Add glucose if using and stir well. Glucose thickens the ganache.
5. Leave to cool in the saucepan.
6. If making orange liqueur-flavoured chocolate ganache, stir in orange liqueur and orange oil when ganache has cooled.
7. Transfer ganache to a bowl, cover with cling wrap and refrigerate. Alternatively, keep ganache in a piping bag secured with a rubber band and refrigerate. The ganache can keep for up to 1 week in the refrigerator.
8. Before using, remove from refrigerator and allow to thaw to room temperature.
9. If ganache is kept in a bowl, quickly whisk with a metal fork or spatula before spreading over cupcakes. If ganache is in a piping bag, lightly press piping bag a few times so that ganache is of a smooth consistency before piping it over the cupcakes.

Note

- I always use heavy cream with a fat percentage of at least 38%, as it guarantees the ganache will be of a desired consistency and volume. If using heavy cream with a fat percentage lower than 38%, you might need to adjust the amounts of ingredients listed here, or the ganache might be too watery. Adjust amount of heavy cream as desired. Add less if you prefer a thicker ganache. For a runnier consistency, use up to 190 g (6$^{4}/_{5}$ oz) heavy cream.
- The amount of fat content in the heavy cream affects the consistency of the ganache. The higher the fat content, the thicker the ganache.
- A slightly thicker consistency is easier for spreading on cupcakes. If too runny, ganache will drip down the cupcakes.
- Adding more honey gives a sweeter taste and a runnier consistency.
- Use semi-sweet chocolate couverture, which has 50–70% cocoa. The resultant taste of the ganache has a wide appeal in my experience. Chocolate with more than 70% cocoa tastes more bitter and is usually an acquired taste.
- I suggest preparing this in bulk and keeping it in the fridge for up to 1 week. It can be served with fruits, biscuits or anything that you fancy.

Caution

- The heavy cream should not fill more than half the saucepan so that it does not overflow when boiling. There should also be sufficient room to whisk the ganache after adding chocolate couverture.

White Chocolate Ganache for 12–15 cupcakes

White chocolate ganache is perfect over light coloured cupcakes. White chocolate can be too sweet for some, but appropriate flavourings will render this ganache very appealing!

Heavy cream 125 g (4$\frac{1}{2}$ oz)

White chocolate couverture 300 g (10$\frac{1}{2}$ oz), chopped

1. Heat heavy cream in a saucepan and bring to a slow boil. Be careful not the burn or overheat the cream.
2. Reduce heat and using a whisk, stir in white chocolate couverture until it melts into the cream. Remove from heat and leave to cool in the saucepan.
3. Once cooled, store in a bowl covered with cling wrap or in a piping bag secured with a rubber band. Chill until needed. The ganache can keep for up to 1 week in the refrigerator.
4. Before using, remove from refrigerator and allow to thaw to room temperature. If ganache is kept in a bowl, quickly whisk with a metal fork or spatula before spreading over cupcakes. If ganache is too hard, warm it up in a microwave oven or leave it in a warm place.

Note

- Use up to 150 g (5$\frac{1}{3}$ oz) heavy cream if you prefer a softer consistency.
- A few drops of peppermint essential oil or essence adds a refreshing taste to this lethally rich frosting.

Cream Cheese Frosting for 15–20 cupcakes

Cream cheese frosting is a must in any baker's repertoire. The slightly tart taste of the cheese balances well with sweet bakes and cakes. The recipe here does not use butter, but if you prefer a softer consistency, a little butter wouldn't hurt.

Cream cheese 500 g (1 lb 1$\frac{1}{2}$ oz), at room temperature

Vanilla extract 1$\frac{1}{2}$ tsp

Icing (confectioner's) sugar 8 Tbsp or to taste, sifted

1. Combine cream cheese and vanilla extract in an electric mixer with a paddle attachment. Beat at high speed for 3 minutes or until soft and fluffy.

2. Add icing sugar and beat at low speed until everything is well blended. Do not over beat as the cream cheese can become grainy.

3. The frosting can be used immediately, although it is recommended to chill before use. To store, cover with cling wrap and keep refrigerated until needed. Refrigerated cream cheese frosting can be kept up to 5 days.

VARIATIONS

- For lemon-flavoured cream cheese, omit vanilla extract and replace with the juice of 1 lemon.
- To make port-infused cream cheese, add up to 3 Tbsp port syrup (page 140) or fresh port. This can be done at Step 1.
- If you like your cream cheese frosting to be soft and with a hint of butter, replace 100 g (3$\frac{1}{2}$ oz) cream cheese with butter.
- To make salted cream cheese, mix in $\frac{1}{2}$ tsp salt just before frosting the cupcakes.

Note

- Sifting icing sugar reduces beating time and minimises lumps.
- Add the icing sugar gradually and taste the frosting before adding more sugar according to taste.
- Before using, remove from refrigerator and let it thaw to room temperature. Whisk with a fork before using.

Mascarpone Frostings

Simple Mascarpone Frosting for 12–15 cupcakes

Mascarpone cheese 250 g (9 oz)

Icing (confectioner's) sugar 50 g (1^2/$_3$ oz)

1. Beat mascarpone cheese and half the sugar in an electric mixer until soft and creamy. Taste and add more sugar as desired.
2. Use immediately or cover with cling wrap and chill in the refrigerator for up to 2 days.

More Elaborate Mascarpone Frosting for 20–24 cupcakes

Heavy cream 200 g (7 oz)

Mascarpone cheese 250 g (9 oz)

Icing (confectioner's) sugar 50 g (1^2/$_3$ oz)

1. Beat heavy cream until stiff peaks form.
2. In a separate bowl, beat mascarpone cheese and half the sugar until soft and creamy. Taste and add more sugar as desired.
3. Fold whipped heavy cream into mascarpone cheese and continue beating until well incorporated.
4. Use immediately or cover with cling wrap and chill in the refrigerator for up to 2 days.

This Italian cheese is lighter (with a lower fat content) and slightly sweeter than cream cheese. It has a creamy consistency, which makes it easy to spoon over cupcakes. It is often more expensive than cream cheese, but it's a treat that is well worth it!

Buttercream Frosting for 12–15 cupcakes

Unsalted butter or vegetable shortening 200 g (7 oz)

Flavouring of choice (page 154)

Icing (confectioner's) sugar 200 g (7 oz), sifted

Water 2–3 Tbsp

Food colouring (optional) a few drops

1. Beat butter or vegetable shortening in an electric mixer for about 2–3 minutes on medium speed.
2. Add flavouring of choice and continue beating.
3. Add icing sugar and continue beating until all ingredients are well combined.
4. Gradually add water, 1 Tbsp at a time, to achieve desired consistency.
5. If adding colour, add a few drops of food colouring and beat until the desired colour is achieved.
6. Use immediately or store accordingly.

Note

- If using butter, take it out of the refrigerator 10–15 minutes before use. Cut into cubes for easier mixing.
- Add more icing sugar if buttercream is too wet. If too dry, add more water. Milk or heavy cream can also be used in place of water.
- If buttercream is too sweet, add up to $1/2$ tsp salt and blend thoroughly.
- Always sift icing sugar so that it blends quickly with butter or vegetable shortening. Sifting also minimises lumps.
- Do not overbeat buttercream as it may become grainy.
- To store buttercream frosting made using butter, cover it with cling wrap or place in an air tight container and refrigerate for up to 1 week.
- To store buttercream frosting made using vegetable shortening, place in an air tight container. It can keep for up to 1 week. There is no need to refrigerate, but keep frosting in a cool place.
- When using buttercream that has been stored away, always use a fork or small metal spatula to whisk it quickly before using.

Buttercream frostings are de rigueur toppings for cupcakes. Cupcakes that have no frostings are as good as incomplete, naked in the world of fashion or worse, plain boring! I have suggested recipes for various flavours on page 154, but you are free to experiment with other flavours. Use butter with at least 80% cream, vegetable shortening (I recommend Criso), or a combination of both. In hot and humid weather, buttercream made with butter has a tendency to 'melt'.

NAME OF FROSTING	FLAVOURING	OPTIONAL
Bailey's Irish Cream	**Bailey's Irish Cream liqueur** 3 Tbsp	Use black coffee in place of water.
Banana	**Vanilla extract** 1 tsp **Banana flavouring** 1 tsp	Add 50 g (1 2/3 oz) well mashed ripe bananas. The coarse texture does not allow for easy piping. Use a spoon to spread over cupcakes instead.
Brandy	**Vanilla extract** 1 tsp **Brandy** 3 tsp	Use more brandy if desired; omit water.
Coca-Cola	**Vanilla extract** 1 tsp **Coca-Cola** 5 tsp	Omit water. Add 1 Tbsp unsweetened cocoa powder, sifted.
Lemon	**Lemon oil** 1 tsp *or* **lemon essential oil** 3–5 drops	Use lemon juice in place of water, and add 2 Tbsp store-bought lemon curd.
Lemon-mint	**Peppermint essence** 1/2 tsp *and* **lemon oil** 1/2 tsp *or* **Peppermint essential oil** 3 drops *and* **lemon essential oil** 3 drops	Use lemon juice in place of water. Add 1 tsp chopped mint leaves.
Orange	**Vanilla extract** 1 tsp **Orange oil** 1 tsp *or* **orange essential oil** 3–5 drops	Add 3 Tbsp orange juice in place of water.
Peppermint	**Peppermint essence** 1 tsp *or* **peppermint essential oil** 3–5 drops	
Rum-spiked Coca-Cola	**Vanilla extract** 1 tsp **Coca-Cola** 3 tsp **Rum** 2 tsp	Omit water. Add 1 Tbsp unsweetened cocoa powder, sifted.
Stout	**Vanilla extract** 1 Tbsp **Stout** 5 Tbsp	Omit water.
Raspberry	**Vanilla extract** 1 tsp **Seedless raspberry jam** 3–4 Tbsp	
Vanilla	**Vanilla extract** 1 tsp	Add 1/2 tsp almond essence.
Vanilla-orange liqueur	**Vanilla extract** 1 tsp **Orange liqueur** 3 Tbsp	Use more liqueur if desired; omit water.
Whisky	**Vanilla extract** 1 tsp **Whisky** 3 Tbsp	Use more whisky if desired; omit water.
White Chocolate	**White chocolate ganache** (page 148) 1 portion **Vanilla buttercream** (see above) 1 portion	

Strawberry Buttercream for 12–15 cupcakes

This tastes just like ice cream thanks to the puréed strawberries! Choose really red strawberries as they give the buttercream a nice natural blush of pink. And there is no need to add water as the strawberries already contain enough moisture. You can also substitute strawberries with other fruits such as peaches or raspberries.

Fresh strawberries 50 g ($1^{2}/_{3}$ oz), hulled

Unsalted butter or vegetable shortening 125 g ($4^{1}/_{2}$ oz)

Salt a pinch

Vanilla extract $^{1}/_{2}$ tsp

Icing (confectioner's) sugar 200 g (7 oz), sifted

1. Process strawberries in a blender to get about 4 Tbsp puréed strawberries. Set aside.
2. Beat butter or vegetable shortening, salt and vanilla extract in an electric mixer for 2–3 minutes on medium speed.
3. Add icing sugar and continue to mix until ingredients are well combined.
4. Gradually add puréed strawberry 1 Tbsp at a time, and stop once you have achieved the desired consistency. The buttercream should be dense, moist (not wet) and fluffy.

Note

- To give it an alcoholic twist, add 1 Tbsp brandy and 2 Tbsp champagne at step 2.

Chocolate Buttercream for 12–15 cupcakes

Cocoa powder gives this chocolate buttercream its desired colour and taste.

Unsalted butter or vegetable shortening 200 g (7 oz)

Vanilla extract 2 tsp

Icing (confectioner's) sugar 200 g (7 oz) + more if desired, sifted

Cocoa powder 85 g (3 oz), sifted

Water or milk 4 Tbsp

Salt (optional) a pinch

1. Beat butter or vegetable shortening in an electric mixer for 2–3 minutes on medium speed.
2. Add vanilla extract and continue beating.
3. Add icing sugar and cocoa powder, and continue beating until all ingredients are well combined.
4. Gradually add water or milk, 1 Tbsp at a time, to achieve desired consistency. You can also add salt to enhance the taste. Use immediately or store in the refrigerator for up to 1 week.

Custard Cream for 12–15 cupcakes

This is easy to make, and its creamy taste and texture goes well with many bakes and sweets.

Full cream milk 250 ml (8 fl oz / 1 cup)

Caster sugar 50 g (1^2/$_3$ oz)

Vanilla extract 1 tsp

Egg yolks from 2 eggs

Cornflour (cornstarch) 25 g (^{4}/$_5$ oz)

Unsalted butter 1^1/$_2$ Tbsp

1. Heat milk, half the sugar and vanilla extract in a saucepan, stirring occasionally with a wooden spoon.
2. In a separate bowl, beat egg yolks, remaining sugar and cornflour. Add to the milk mixture.
3. Bring to the boil again, whisking constantly until mixture is smooth and thick. Remove from heat and whisk in butter.
4. Leave to cool before using.

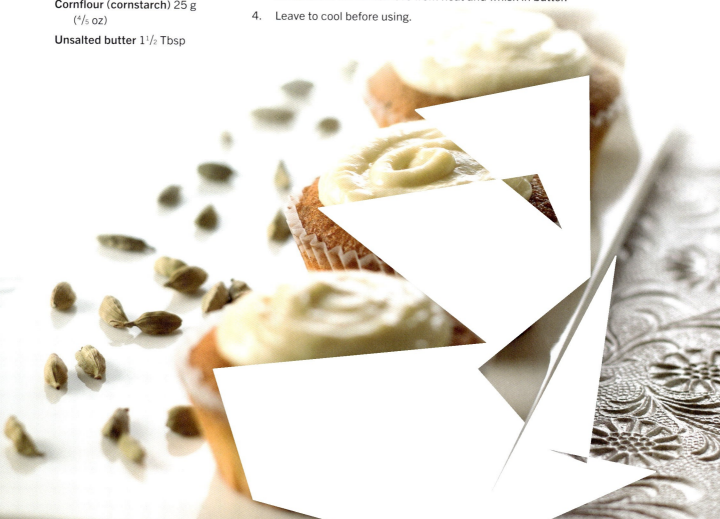

Royal Icing for 12–15 cupcakes

Royal icing is primarily made of icing sugar and will harden to a stiff consistency if left to dry. It is typically used to decorate gingerbread cookies or fancy wedding cakes.

Icing (confectioner's) sugar
200 g (7 oz), sifted

Water as needed

Meringue powder (optional)
1 Tbsp

1. Place icing sugar in a bowl and using a whisk, gradaully mix in water, $1/2$ tsp at a time, until desired consistency is reached. It should spread well and not be too stiff or runny.

2. Use immediately. If not, cover with a moist cloth to prevent it from hardening. You can also store it in an air tight container in the refrigerator for up to 1 week.

3. Before using, whisk with a fork or small metal spatula until smooth. You may add a bit of water to soften the icing if need be.

Note
- If royal icing becomes too runny, add more icing sugar.
- If desired, replace water with fruit juices or flavourings of your choice.
- If royal icing is too runny, dip the top of the cupcakes into the icing to get an even but thin layer on them.
- Meringue powder is often added to making royal icing really stiff. This type of royal icing is very suitable for elaborate decorations on celebratory cakes. If using, incorporate at step 1, before mixing in water.

Whipped Topping Cream for 12–15 cupcakes

This is really easy to make and great for bakers who want convenience! Layer the whipped topping cream over cupcakes and top with slices of fruits or berries or a light dusting of cocoa powder.

Topping cream *or* **non-dairy whipping cream** 200 g (7 oz)

Preferred flavouring or alcohol to taste

1. Using an electric mixer fitted with a whisk attachment in an electric mixer, beat cream at high speed for a few minutes. The cream will gather volume and form soft peaks.
2. Add flavouring or alcohol of choice, and ensure it is well incorporated.
3. The longer you beat the cream, the more air will be incorporated, thus making the whipped cream stiff. Be careful though, prolonged whisking will render the whipped cream grainy.

Note

- While whipped topping cream keeps really well, it is better to cover with cling wrap before storing in the refrigerator. If kept properly, whipped topping cream will keep for up to 5 days. Before use, whisk the whipping cream with a spatula.
- If using whipping cream, this frosting should be kept refrigerated until needed.

Whipped Heavy Cream for 12–15 cupcakes

Heavy cream 200 g (7 oz)

Icing (confectioner's) sugar to taste

Preferred flavouring as desired

1. Using an electric mixer fitted with a whisk attachment, beat heavy cream at high speed for a few minutes.
2. Gradually add icing sugar, 1 Tbsp at a time. Taste and add more sugar until desired sweetness is achieved.
3. Continue to whisk until soft peaks form. Add desired flavouring if using.

Note

- The higher the fat content, the easier it is to whip the heavy cream up to form. The longer you beat the cream, the more air will be incorporated, thus making the whipped cream stiff. Be careful though, prolonged whisking will render the whipped cream grainy.
- If not using immediately, cover with cling wrap before storing in the refrigerator. This will keep for up to 5 days. Before use, whisk with a spatula.
- Heavy cream should always be refrigerated until needed.

This can be tricky to make, but using chilled heavy cream and chilling the mixing bowl and whisk for 15 minutes before using will help the cream whip up more easily.

Condensed Milk Glaze for 12–15 cupcakes

Those with a sweet tooth can literally eat this on its own!

Unsalted butter 30 g (1 oz), softened
Sweetened condensed milk 4 Tbsp
Salt (optional) a pinch
Icing (confectioner's) sugar 35 g (1¼ oz), sifted

1. In a bowl, mix softened butter and condensed milk with a spatula. Mix in salt if using.
2. Add sugar, 1 Tbsp at a time, and continue mixing until all the ingredients are well incorporated. The glaze should be thick and smooth.
3. Use immediately.
4. If storing away, cover with cling wrap and refrigerate. This will keep for up to 1 week.

Stout Glaze for 12–15 cupcakes

Icing (confectioner's) sugar 200 g (7 oz), sifted
Stout 2–3 Tbsp

1. Place icing sugar in a bowl. Using a whisk, gradually mix in stout, ½ tsp at a time, until a smooth consistency is achieved. The glaze should be runny.
2. If the glaze is too runny, add more icing sugar.
3. If glaze is too stiff, add more stout.

Kiwi Glaze for 12–15 cupcakes

This glaze is cooked over heat, and is clear or translucent.
You can use other types of fruits to make this glaze.

Caster sugar 55 g (2 oz)
Water 4 Tbsp
Kiwi 1, peeled and cut into bite-size pieces

1. Heat sugar and water in a saucepan over medium heat, stirring occasionally to prevent sugar from burning. Once mixture comes to a boil, add kiwi fruit pieces.
2. Lower heat and allow it to simmer for 5 minutes, or until mixture has reduced and thickened.
3. Remove from heat and leave to cool before use.

Note
- You can use this method to make alcoholic fruit glazes as well.
- Prepare glaze as above with your choice of fruits. Allow glaze to reduce. When glaze is cooling down, add your preferred alcohol (up to 2 Tbsp) and stir well, ensuring it is well incorporated. Cool completely before use.

Orange Glaze for 12–15 cucpakes

This recipe does not require any cooking, and it is easy to make.

Icing (confectioner's sugar)
150 g (5$\frac{1}{3}$ oz), sifted

Orange zest grated from
$\frac{1}{2}$ orange

Orange juice 3 Tbsp

1. Place icing sugar in a bowl. Using a whisk, gradually mix in orange zest and juice, $\frac{1}{2}$ tsp at a time, until a smooth consistency is achieved. The glaze should be runny.
2. Add more icing sugar to thicken glaze, or more orange juice if you like a runnier glaze.

Note

- You can replace orange with other kinds of citrus fruits if you prefer.

Orange Vodka Glaze for 12–15 cucpakes

Icing (confectioner's sugar)
150 g (5$\frac{1}{3}$ oz), sifted

Orange oil $\frac{1}{4}$ tsp

Vodka 3 Tbsp

1. Place icing sugar in a bowl. Using a whisk, gradually mix in orange oil, followed by vodka, $\frac{1}{2}$ tsp at a time, until a smooth consistency is achieved. The glaze should be runny.
2. Add more icing sugar to thicken glaze, or more vodka if you prefer a runnier glaze.

Note

- To make tequila-spiked orange glaze, replace vodka with tequila.

Tofu Frosting for 15–20 cupcakes

This is a very healthy and tasty frosting. You may also use this as a salad dressing.

Soft tofu 200 g (7 oz)
Lemon juice 1 tsp
Vanilla extract ½ tsp
Icing (confectioner's) sugar up to 3 Tbsp

1. Pat dry tofu with paper towels.
2. Break up tofu and place in a blender. Add lemon juice and vanilla extract. Blend for 30 seconds.
3. Add icing sugar, 1 Tbsp at a time, tasting as you mix. Adjust amount of icing sugar to taste.

Note

- For a thicker consistency, use firm tofu.
- Depending on the water content of the tofu used, this frosting can be soft and wet. Consider replacing lemon juice with 3 drops of lemon essential oil; this way, you can give it a nice citrusy twist without adding excess liquid.

Coconut-Rum Frosting for 12–15 cupcakes

Icing (confectioner's) sugar 300 g (10½ oz), sifted

Coconut-flavoured rum 1 Tbsp

Store-bought thick coconut cream 85 ml (2½ fl oz / ⅓ cup)

1. Whisk icing sugar and coconut-flavoured rum quickly in a bowl.
2. Gradually adding coconut cream while whisking.
3. The frosting should be opaque with a smooth and runny consistency.

Sea Salt Caramel Frosting for 12–15 cupcakes

Unsalted butter 50 g (1⅔ oz)

Brown sugar 80 g (2⅘ oz)

Golden syrup 1 Tbsp

Heavy cream 30 g (1 oz)

Sea salt ½ tsp

Buttercream (page 152) 1 portion

1. Prepare caramel. Heat butter, brown sugar, golden syrup and heavy cream in a saucepan and bring to a gentle boil, stirring occasionally with a wooden spoon.
2. Once boiling, turn heat up and let it boil for another 2–3 minutes.
3. Remove from heat and allow the caramel to cool down a bit. It should be warm but of a pouring consistency.
4. The buttercream should already be prepared and sitting in the cake mixer. Slowly pour caramel into buttercream. Beat at high speed until well blended. Add salt and mix well.
5. Use immediately or store covered in the refrigerator for up to 5 days.

Note
- Add more icing sugar if frosting is too wet and more heavy cream if it is too stiff.

No-Bake Meringue for 12–15 cupcakes

This recipe is suitable for children and pregnant women, or those with health concerns, because it uses meringue powder, which is the best alternative to raw egg whites. When preparing this meringue, all equipment and your hands must be cleaned well and free from any grease. If not, the volume of the meringue will be affected.

Meringue powder 1 Tbsp

Water 4 Tbsp

Caster sugar 150 g (5$^{1}/_{3}$ oz)

Lemon juice (or other flavouring of choice) $^{1}/_{2}$ tsp

1. Put meringue powder, water and half the sugar in a large mixing bowl. Using an electric mixer fitted with a whisk attachment, whisk at high speed for about 5 minutes.
2. Slowly add remaining sugar and continue whisking at high speed for another 5 minutes.
3. Test by rubbing some of the meringue between your fingers. It should be smooth. If you still feel the sugar granules, continue beating as the sugar has not fully dissolved. Stop beating once meringue is stiff and dry.
4. Add lemon juice or other flavouring of choice and whisk for 1–2 minutes. Use immediately.

Note

- No-bake meringue tends to 'sweat' once it is kept in the open for too long.
- When making meringue, make sure that everything (the spoons, pots, etc.) and your hands are totally clean, because the slightest bit of oil can affect the meringue.
- If making rose-scented no-bake meringue, replace lemon juice with 2 drops of rose essential oil or $^{1}/_{2}$ tsp rose essence.
- You can use this to make meringue cookies if you like:
  1. Add desired flavouring and mix well, or fold in chocolate and nuts if desired.
  2. Preheat oven to 125°C (275°F).
  3. Pipe or spoon little dollops of meringue on a baking tray lined with parchment paper. Place baking tray on the highest shelf and bake for 2 hours.
  4. Meringue cookies should be easily removed from parchment paper. If not, pop them back into the oven for another 30 minutes. Turn off the heat and allow meringue cookies to sit in the oven with the door slightly ajar. Leave them to bake in the residual heat for another hour.

Weights and Measures

Quantities for this book are given in Metric and American (spoon and cup) measures. Standard spoon and cup measurements used are: 1 tsp = 5 ml, 1 dsp = 10 ml, 1 Tbsp = 15 ml, 1 cup = 250 ml. All measures are level unless otherwise stated.

LIQUID AND VOLUME MEASURES

Metric	Imperial	American
5 ml	1/6 fl oz	1 tsp
10 ml	1/3 fl oz	1 dsp
15 ml	1/2 fl oz	1 Tbsp
60 ml	2 fl oz	1/4 cup (4 Tbsp)
85 ml	2 1/2 fl oz	1/3 cup
90 ml	3 fl oz	3/8 cup (6 Tbsp)
125 ml	4 fl oz	1/2 cup
180 ml	6 fl oz	3/4 cup
250 ml	8 fl oz	1 cup
300 ml	10 fl oz (1/2 pint)	1 1/4 cups
375 ml	12 fl oz	1 1/2 cups
435 ml	14 fl oz	1 3/4 cups
500 ml	16 fl oz	2 cups
625 ml	20 fl oz (1 pint)	2 1/2 cups
750 ml	24 fl oz (1 1/5 pints)	3 cups
1 litre	32 fl oz (1 3/5 pints)	4 cups
1.25 litres	40 fl oz (2 pints)	5 cups
1.5 litres	48 fl oz (2 2/5 pints)	6 cups
2.5 litres	80 fl oz (4 pints)	10 cups

DRY MEASURES

Metric	Imperial
30 g	1 ounce
45 g	1 1/2 ounces
55 g	2 ounces
70 g	2 1/2 ounces
85 g	3 ounces
100 g	3 1/2 ounces
110 g	4 ounces
125 g	4 1/2 ounces
140 g	5 ounces
280 g	10 ounces
450 g	16 ounces (1 pound)
500 g	1 pound, 1 1/2 ounces
700 g	1 1/2 pounds
800 g	1 3/4 pounds
1 kg	2 pounds, 3 ounces
1.5 kg	3 pounds, 4 1/2 ounces
2 kg	4 pounds, 6 ounces

OVEN TEMPERATURE

	°C	°F	Gas Regulo
Very slow	120	250	1
Slow	150	300	2
Moderately slow	160	325	3
Moderate	180	350	4
Moderately hot	190/200	370/400	5/6
Hot	210/220	410/440	6/7
Very hot	230	450	8
Super hot	250/290	475/550	9/10

LENGTH

Metric	Imperial
0.5 cm	1/4 inch
1 cm	1/2 inch
1.5 cm	3/4 inch
2.5 cm	1 inch

ABBREVIATION

tsp	teaspoon
Tbsp	tablespoon
dsp	dessertspoon
g	gram
kg	kilogram
ml	millilitre